CUBA AND THE UNITED STATES

CUBA AND THE UNITED STATES

TROUBLED NEIGHBORS

EDWARD F. DOLAN, JR.
AND
MARGARET M. SCARIANO

FRANKLIN WATTS | AN IMPACT BOOK | 1987
NEW YORK | LONDON | TORONTO | SYDNEY

327.73
Dol

Map by Vantage Art

Photographs courtesy of:
The New York Public Library Picture Collection: p. 21;
The Bettmann Archive: pp. 36, 39;
Culver Pictures, Inc.: p. 42;
UPI/Bettmann Newsphotos: pp. 57, 71, 82, 94, 118;
U.S. Air Force: pp. 97, 98.

Library of Congress Cataloging-in-Publication Data

Dolan, Edward F.
Cuba and the United States

(An Impact book)
Bibliography: p.
Includes index.
Summary: Traces the history of relations between Cuba and the United States from the Revolutionary War to the present day.
1. United States—Foreign Relations—Cuba. 2. Cuba—Foreign Relations—United States. [1. United States—Foreign Relations—Cuba. 2. Cuba—Foreign Relations—United States] I. Scariano, Margaret. II. Title.
E183.8.C9D57 1987   327.7307291   86-23347
ISBN 0-531-10327-7

Copyright © 1987 by Edward F. Dolan, Jr.,
and Margaret M. Scariano
All rights reserved
Printed in the United States of America
6 5 4 3 2 1

CONTENTS

Chapter One
Island in a New World
11

Chapter Two
Matters of Influence
24

Chapter Three
War and Entanglement
35

Chapter Four
Two Dictators
51

Chapter Five
A New Revolt, a New Leader
63

Chapter Six
Total War—And Victory
75

Chapter Seven
Troubled Neighbors: From Suspicions to Missiles
84

Chapter Eight
Troubled Neighbors: Castro's Failed Dream
101

Chapter Nine
Troubled Neighbors: Cuba and the United States Today
111

Recommended Reading List 123

Index 125

The authors wish to thank
Christopher Mitchell, Associate
Professor, New York University,
for reading this book in manuscript
form and making many fine editorial
suggestions and comments.

CUBA AND THE UNITED STATES

1
ISLAND IN A NEW WORLD

On a sunny October 27, 1492, Christopher Columbus dropped anchor off a sandy coast that stretched across his path for as far as the eye could see in either direction. With his three small ships—the *Santa María,* the *Niña,* and the *Pinta*—the explorer had just sailed across the Atlantic Ocean from Spain in search of a westward sea route to the rich Orient. He was certain that this warm and humid day had brought him to his destination.

Columbus was mistaken. The Orient still lay thousands of miles beyond the cloud-flecked western horizon. What he had come upon was an island never before seen by a European. Future explorations would reveal it to be a long and slender land mass—measuring about 2,500 miles (4,000 km) all around and, on average, 60 miles (97 km) across. When it was finally added to the maps of the world, the outline of the newly found land would look something like a thin animal sitting on its haunches and leaning far forward, as if trying to nibble at a tasty morsel just out of its reach. Within that outline, explorers would find 44,218 square miles (114,525 sq. km) of highly varied terrain.

Just how varied? Columbus and the other European explorers who followed him in the succeeding years would discover bays and snug inlets all along the island's shoreline. They would come upon sandy lowlands and swamps on its southern coast, and steep, rocky cliffs along its northern shores. Venturing inland, they would see that the island divided itself between flat, yet rolling lands and rugged hills and thickly forested mountains, the highest of which—Turquino—rose to 6,560 feet (2,000 m). Everywhere, rivers and streams made their way to the sea. And, everywhere, because the soil was rich in limestone and washed so often with warm rains, the land was fertile, yielding more than eight thousand varieties of plant life.

On rowing ashore for the first time, Columbus met a group of brown-skinned natives. When he learned something of their language, he found that they were Arawak Indians and that their people had inhabited the island for generations. They called their homeland Cubanacan.

Over the coming years, that word would be shortened and would become the name of the island as we know it today—Cuba.

A NEW WORLD

In searching for a sea route to the Orient, Columbus was testing a theory that Europe's leading scientists and navigators had held for years—that the world was a globe and that the Far East could be reached by sailing west across the Atlantic Ocean. Commanding eighty-eight seamen who feared that they would sail off the edge of the world at any moment or fall prey to some horrible sea monster, Columbus was in the vanguard of the adventurers who proved the theory to be correct.

What Columbus did not know when he departed Spain on August 3, 1492—indeed, what no one in the Europe of his day realized—was that a "New World" stood in his path and that, on its far side, lay a vast ocean that had to be crossed before a ship could drop anchor off a Far Eastern shore. Making up that New World were two giant continents that in the future would be called North and South America. Separated by water for much of their widths, these giant land masses were joined at their western ends by the sometimes-thick and sometimes-narrow strip of land known today as Central America.

His voyage carried Columbus out of the Atlantic Ocean and into the waters separating the two continents. Here, he came upon a cluster of islands, which as a look at a modern map shows, arc northwest across the Caribbean Ocean from South America's Venezuela to Florida in the United States. Formed by the peaks of an underwater mountain chain and named the West Indies by Columbus, they include such small land masses as the Windward and Leeward islands. Ranking as larger members are the islands of Puerto Rico, Jamaica, and Hispaniola (the home of Haiti and the Dominican Republic). The largest member of the family is Cuba.

Columbus's voyage was financed by Queen Isabella of Spain. As he did wherever else he traveled, the explorer took possession of the island for Spain when he landed at Cuba. Destined to remain in Spanish hands for more than four centuries, Cuba quickly emerged as Spain's most important holding in the New World. There were two reasons for this, both of which can be seen by looking again at a modern map.

First, Cuba lies at the northwestern edge of the Caribbean Ocean, right at the entrance to the Gulf of Mexico. Because of its location, the island served as a fine springboard for the expeditions that, in the early 1500s, explored the northern coasts of South America, plunged into the jungles of the Isthmus of Panama and sighted the Pacific Ocean, and subdued the Aztec Indians of Mexico, turning their country into a Spanish possession. Conversely—and

of even greater importance to Spain—Cuba served as the main base from which the New World's fantastic riches in gold and then foodstuffs were shipped back to the motherland. The city of Havana (*Habana* in Spanish) took shape near the island's northwestern tip. It became the chief point of departure for the shipments for home aboard galleons—and a major naval base, supplying provisions for the fleets of warships needed to protect the gold-laden galleons.

Second, of all the Caribbean islands, Cuba is the one lying closest to North America. Cuba and its continental neighbor are separated by the Straits of Florida and, at one point, are but a mere 90 miles (145 km) apart. Consequently, the greatest Spanish names in the early exploration of the North American continent all have a place in the island's history.

For example, one of the very earliest explorers, Juan Ponce de León, visited Cuba in 1493 while serving with Columbus on his second voyage to the New World. In 1509, de León conquered the island of Puerto Rico and was appointed its governor. While there, he heard the Indian legend of a magical fountain somewhere far to the north, a fountain whose waters had the power to make all who drank them young again. The governor was in his fifties at the time and feared that his life was drawing to a close. In 1513, he set sail to locate the fountain and reclaim his youth. On Easter Sunday, his ships dropped anchor off a sun-drenched land of such beauty that he christened it Florida, from the Spanish term *Pascua Florida*, meaning "Flowery Easter."

De León explored both the east and west coasts of Florida and, not once glimpsing the magical fountain, sailed away in disappointment. Seven years later, on orders from the king of Spain, he returned with the intention of establishing a colony there. But, soon after landing, he and his men were attacked by natives. In the fierce engagement, de León was badly wounded. His men carried him back to their ships and fled to Cuba. De León died at Havana a few weeks later, in June, 1521.

Another of the era's most famous adventurers—Hernando de Soto—served for a time as governor of Cuba. In 1539, he departed Havana with a force of six hundred men and sailed to the west coast of de León's Florida. For the next two years, de Soto marched northward into what are now the Carolinas and then westward through today's Alabama, at last becoming the first outsider to see the Mississippi River. From there, he continued on to the Ozark Mountains and the Red River.

Interested only in finding gold and silver, de Soto cared little about befriending the Indians he met along the way. Instead, often treating them cruelly, he earned their enmity. By the time the Mississippi came into view, de Soto had lost a third of his force in skirmishes with the Indians. De Soto himself fell ill during the explorations west of the Mississippi and died upon his return to the river. His men lowered his body into its waters and then made their way home.

In the 1540s, Francisco Vásquez de Coronado set sail from Cuba to become the Spanish governor of Mexico. As had happened earlier to de León, Coronado encountered an Indian legend soon after his arrival. This one spoke of distant cities made of gold. In a fruitless search for the cities, Coronado explored north into today's Texas, New Mexico, Kansas, and Arizona, where he became the first European to see the Grand Canyon.

LINKED HISTORIES

De León, de Soto, and Coronado rank as important figures in the history of exploration because they were among the first Europeans to venture onto the North American continent, the future home of Canada and the United States. For the purposes of this book—the story of Cuba and the United States as neighbors—the three men are especially important. They were the very first to link the histories of the two countries together.

Ever since those long-ago days, the histories of Cuba and the United States have remained closely linked—at times happily and at other times, as is the case today, unhappily. The links that bind them are three:

Though vastly different in physical size and in the makeup of their populations, the two nations bear a number of similarities in their histories.

Throughout their histories, the two have influenced each other politically and economically.

The two countries have been at odds for some thirty years now and have suffered enduring tensions—and moments of frightening crisis—because they hold diametrically opposed ideological views, with the United States being a free-world nation, and Cuba a communist state.

In the coming pages, we look at each of these links, beginning with the similarities to be found in the histories of the two countries.

A DIFFERENCE AND A SAMENESS

The two neighbors—one an island of Spanish-speaking people, the other an English-speaking continental nation—are indeed different. For its part, the United States is a sprawling land of fifty states, with its area of 3,536,955 square miles (5,694,498 sq. km) making it the world's fourth largest country (after the Soviet Union, China, and Canada). Its 232 million people constitute the world's most varied population. Their roots can be traced to every part of the globe.

On the other hand, Cuba ranks among the smallest of nations. Divided into fourteen provinces, it is a little larger in area than Portugal and about the size of Pennsylvania. Its population of approximately 9.8 million is also among the world's smallest—smaller than that of the tiny island of

Sri Lanka in the Indian Ocean—and far less varied than that of the United States. Whites of Spanish descent make up about 73 percent of the people, blacks account for 12 percent, and a mixed black-and-Spanish group (called *mestizos*) for 15 percent. There are some thirty thousand Orientals (*amarillos*) living in Cuba. The island is also home for a few people of French descent. Their forebears, coming from nearby French possessions in the late 1700s, helped to launch Cuba's sugar industry.

But, as different as the two countries are, they have histories that are markedly similar in at least five respects.

1. Foreign Domination

Prior to becoming independent nations, both countries were held by foreign powers. From the day of its discovery until the early twentieth century, Cuba served as a Spanish possession. Throughout the 1600s, Spain fought wars with the British, French, and Dutch to protect its rich New World holdings. In 1762, the British attacked Cuba and captured Havana after a lengthy siege. The invaders held the city for about a year and then returned it to Spain in trade for the Spanish holdings in Florida.

Spain, France, the Netherlands, and Great Britain—all struggled for a foothold in the future United States, with Great Britain at last emerging as the dominant power along the northern Atlantic seaboard while France and Spain flourished in the southern areas.

2. Agricultural Riches

Early on, both Cuba and the future United States proved to be rich agricultural areas. To keep Havana supplied as a major port and naval base, the Spanish quickly developed a thriving agriculture in many parts of the island. They brought in horses, dogs, and cattle. They imported grains and European vegetables for planting and set about growing and harvesting such local foods as cassava (a shrubby plant with a bitter milky juice), sweet potatoes, and plantains (short-stemmed, weedy herbs). In later years, the island became a major world producer of tobacco, coffee, and especially sugar (plus such sugar by-products as molasses, syrups, and industrial alcohol). For a time in the late nineteenth and early twentieth centuries, Cuba was a chief supplier of sugar for the United States. Other important crops of the island included rice, vegetables, pineapples, coconuts, bananas, and citrus fruits. (Note: Cuba also produces such minerals as cobalt, copper, iron, manganese, nickel, and salt.)

On the North American continent, the settlers fanned out to the west and south, growing an increasing number of crops as they went—wheat and all other types of grain products, vegetables, citrus fruits, cotton, and tobacco.

3. Economic Exploitation

Cuba and the future United States suffered the exact same economic exploitation at the hands of their mother countries. This was because each mother country believed that its New World holdings existed solely for the good of the homeland.

Spain at first plundered the New World of gold. Cuba itself was not a source of gold, but only a base for its homeward-bound shipments from other parts of the New World. However, when the island's riches turned out to be agricultural products, the mother country would not allow Cuba to trade with other nations. All Cuban exports had to be transported on Spanish vessels. Further, the Cuban people were forbidden to produce anything that would compete with goods being grown or manufactured in Spain.

From the earliest days of Columbus, Spain kept a tight grip on its New World holdings. But Great Britain allowed its first North American colonies to develop as they pleased. Then, in 1760, a new king—George III—ascended the British throne and called for a policy that would be identical to that used by the Spanish. To enrich the homeland and make it stronger, the English king forbade the British colonies to trade among themselves or with other nations. All their goods had to be sent to England, with British companies then taking them over for further trade. The colonies could have no industries that competed with those in England. They were also told to concentrate on producing goods that would help Britain in the many wars it was fighting as it extended its power to various parts of the world.

These policies angered the people in the Spanish and British holdings, fostering in many the desire for independence.

4. Slaveholders

To meet the agricultural needs of their growing populations at the least cost possible, both Cuba and its northern neighbor early adopted the practice of slavery. The future United States imported its first African slaves in 1619 and put them to work in the tobacco fields of Virginia. Black slaves were to be found working cotton plantations throughout the American South by the nineteenth century. But that century saw the nation become angrily divided over the slavery issue, an issue that finally led to the Civil War and the freeing of slaves in the United States.

Slavery appeared in Cuba during the early 1500s, when the Spanish were establishing settlements throughout the island. An increasing amount of farm labor was

Slaves harvesting and processing sugarcane on a Cuban sugar plantation in the 1600s

soon required to produce the foods needed by the settlements themselves and by the great port and naval base that Havana had by then become.

At first, the island's natives were enslaved for much of the farm work. But the Spanish quickly learned that the Indians were not able to handle the amount of labor that had to be done. The Indians were accustomed to a slower way of life. They were peaceful and could be easily enslaved, but they could not be molded into a highly energetic work force. If driven too hard or if mistreated by harsh overseers, they simply sat down and became ill, often dying. Their plight was such that one Indian chieftain, named Hatuey, led his people in revolt in 1514. In retaliation, the enraged Spanish massacred several hundred Indian workers.

By 1522, there had been so many deaths among the Indians from harsh treatment at Spanish hands—and from diseases unknown in Cuba until the arrival of the Europeans—that the island's Indian population had all but disappeared. Steps had to be taken to replace the natives. The first slaves from Africa were imported. In the years that followed, thousands of African captives arrived to work the island's sugar, coffee, and tobacco fields. The Cuban practice of slavery was ended in the late 1800s, a step that was inspired in great part by the end of slavery in the United States.

5. Revolutionary Heritage

Both Cuba and the United States were born of revolution. The British colonies won their independence and established themselves as a nation in the Revolutionary War of the 1770s. Cuba's independence came early in the twentieth century after decades marked by rebellion. In the mid-twentieth century, the island was the scene of yet another revolution, one that saw Cuba become a communist state under its present leader, Premier Fidel Castro.

And so the two countries, so different in size and racial composition, are linked by five historical similarities. Now let's turn to other ways in which the two are linked. How have they influenced each other politically and economically over the centuries. How have they come to be so at odds in their political beliefs that they are today such troubled neighbors?

For the answers, we must start with the American Revolutionary War and then follow a tide of history forward to the present day.

2

MATTERS OF INFLUENCE

Cuba was the first of the two countries to influence the history of the other, which it did during the American Revolutionary War.

In 1779, when the American Revolution was two years old, Spain joined France and the Netherlands in declaring war on Great Britain. Spain did not go to war to help the American colonists but to win some advantages from her long-time enemy. And win them she did. For one, in the peace treaty that followed the American victory, Spain regained the Florida holdings that it had lost to Britain two decades earlier. As you will recall from chapter one, these had been exchanged for Havana, which the British had captured in 1762.

But exactly what role did Spain's Cuba play in the Revolution? The island served as the springboard for Spanish military expeditions that captured English bases in the Bahama Islands and on the North American mainland at Mobile, Alabama, and Pensacola, Florida. Of even greater importance to the Americans, Spain allowed a

French fleet under Admiral Comte François de Grasse to use Havana as a supply depot. In 1781, this fleet proved to be a significant factor in the final victory of the Revolution. Here is what happened.

For several years, the French had actively assisted the American revolutionaries, supplying them with soldiers, a number of warships, and such military leaders as the young Marquis de Lafayette. In 1781, Lafayette's troops met the English army under General Charles Cornwallis at Green Spring, Virginia. Cornwallis, after almost capturing the youthful Frenchman, moved his men to the city of Yorktown on the shores of Chesapeake Bay, where he knew that British ships could bring him needed supplies from New York City.

But the British ships never arrived. They were prevented from doing so by de Grasse. His fleet sailed in and stationed itself offshore while General George Washington's forces joined Lafayette's troops, took up positions all along the land side of Yorktown, and prepared to attack. Trapped with his back to the bay and unable to obtain supplies from the sea, Cornwallis surrendered, bringing the Revolution to an end and making way for the birth of the United States.

VITAL MEMORY

And so Cuba had played a role in American history. In the years following Yorktown, the memory of the Revolutionary War played a role in Cuban history.

The American Revolution—and the successful French Revolution that followed in the late 1780s and early 1790s—inspired many of Spain's New World holdings to seek their own independence. The Latin American colonists, feeling a growing pride in their lands, were growing weary of Spanish domination. They wanted to be free. They wanted to manage their own affairs. The opening decades of the 1800s witnessed a series of uprisings and political movements that resulted in the formation of new independent nations throughout South America, among them Venezuela in 1811, Chile in 1818, Colombia in 1819, Peru in 1824, Bolivia in 1825, and Ecuador in 1830.

The freedoms that had been won in North America and France also inspired a number of Cubans. In 1822 a young poet named José María de Heredia formed a secret society that called for independence from Spain. The Spanish authorities unearthed the society and put an end to it. De Heredia fled the island, but his writings—urging his countrymen to throw off the yoke of Spanish domination and build a nation for themselves—remained to encourage future revolutionaries.

Actually, for several reasons, the yoke of Spanish domination was not as heavy in de Heredia's day as it had been in earlier times. For one, the old rule of trading only with the mother country had been dropped and Cuba was enjoying a profitable commerce with other nations, chief among them the young United States. The rule against trading with other countries had disappeared back in 1762 when the British had captured and held Havana for about a year. During that time, the British had allowed the Cubans to trade with whomever they wished. Such a lively commerce had taken shape that the Spanish had wisely not ended it when they resumed control of the city.

Further, there had been a growth of democratic ideals in Spain during the early years of the 1800s, a growth that had resulted in a democratic constitution for the country in 1812. Cuba benefited from that constitution. The island was granted freedom of the press, and a greater voice in its affairs, and was allowed to send representatives to the *Cortes*, the Spanish parliament at Madrid.

But, in 1825, there was a sudden change for the worse. This was brought about partly because of the fears that de Heredia's secret society had triggered in the homeland and partly because the Spanish government had come under a new and repressive regime. Spain tightened its grip on Cuba. The Spanish army and a series of governors, called captains-general, took on an iron-fisted control of the island. One captain-general, Miguel de Tacón, suppressed the democratic constitution. Freedom of the press disappeared, and political dissidents were quickly imprisoned. In 1837, Cuba was told that it could no longer send representatives to the *Cortes*. Tyranny reigned.

As could be expected, the new tyranny kindled in many Cubans a deeper desire for freedom and independence. One was a youth, Francisco de Aquero, who came from a well-known and wealthy family; when he was arrested for his revolutionary activities, he was put to death. He proved to be the first in a long line of young and old who sought independence and found death instead. In the next years, secret societies took quiet shape in various parts of the island—in the countryside, in villages and small towns, and in the major cities of Havana, Santiago de Cuba, and Camagüey. When these societies were discovered and smashed by the authorities, their leaders faced immediate execution. Hundreds died while hundreds more fled for their lives, going into hiding or escaping to other nations, among them the United States.

For two basic reasons, all these calls for freedom came to nothing. First, unlike the countries that had waged successful fights for independence in South America, Cuba was a small island; as such, it could be more easily controlled and subdued by Spain than could the nations on a vast continent. Second, most of the Cuban revolutionary leaders were poets, artists, students, and the children of some of the island's wealthiest families. They were idealists who were better at thinking than at action. Though courageously willing to die for their ideals, they simply were not the tough fighters who are needed to trigger a revolution and make it succeed.

As a consequence, after watching so many of its fellow

colonies become independent nations, Cuba remained in Spanish hands at midcentury. But the desire for independence also remained, intensifying daily under the tyrannical army rule. Had you been in Cuba at the time, however, you would have found that the desire for independence had taken three different forms.

To begin, you would have met Cubans who wanted their land to have a greater independence while still continuing to be a Spanish possession. But they wanted the island to be not a mere colony but a self-governing province within the Spanish empire. Many of these people were loyal to Spain because they had been born there.

Next, you would have come upon those who wanted complete independence from the mother country. They yearned to see Cuba become a nation on its own. Many of their number were Cuban-born. And many admired the democratic United States and thought that their dreamed-of nation should be modeled on—and boast the same constitution as—the young country to the north.

Finally, you would have encountered those who wanted to see their island annexed by and made part of the United States. These people were mainly sugar, tobacco, and coffee growers who owned much of Cuba's land. They were slaveowners who were suffering the anger of their many countrymen who had long hated slavery and who now wanted to have it abolished. They were also fearful of the growing rebelliousness that they saw in their slaves. In 1843, these slaveowners had been terrified on learning of a plot to trigger a slave rebellion in the northern province of Matanzas. The authorities had smashed the plot and had executed several of its alleged black and Cuban leaders, among them the gifted mulatto poet, Gabriel de la Concepción Valdes.

In all, these slaveowners felt that they would gain strength by wedding Cuba to a giant nation that contained a number of slave-holding states within its borders.

ANNEXATION:
THE AMERICAN VIEW

The slaveholders were not alone in wanting Cuba to be joined to the United States. The same idea had long been in United States minds. The island was so close at hand—just 90 miles (145 km) off the Florida coast—that it struck many Americans as being a part of their continent and thus a logical candidate for annexation. At the beginning of the 1800s, President Thomas Jefferson had looked on annexation of Cuba as a good idea.

Now, at midcentury, with the United States extending its borders clear across the continent, a step was taken to obtain Cuba. In April, 1854, President Franklin Pierce offered Spain $130 million for the island. It was an offer that was promptly rejected—and then again rejected whenever it was repeated.

A few months later, another step was taken, one that threatened war with the Spanish. The American ambassadors to Spain, France, and Great Britain met in Ostend, Belgium, and drafted a document that became known as the Ostend Manifesto. The ambassadors from these countries were, respectively, Pierre Soulé, John Young Mason, and the future U.S. president, James Buchanan. Their manifesto, which was sent to Secretary of State William Marcy, urged the United States to seize Cuba by force if Spain continued to refuse President Pierce's offer to buy the island.

The manifesto angered not only Spain but also the American antislavery movement that had taken shape in the Northern states and was spreading to other parts of the country. The leaders of the antislavery movement claimed that the idea of seizing Cuba had been born in the slave-holding Southern states. They held that the Southerners hoped to gain strength and offset the antislavery movement by adding a new slave territory to the nation.

Whatever the truth might have been, the idea of buying Cuba or taking it by force eventually came to nothing. The practice of slavery finally split the United States for the five terrible years of the Civil War and ended with that war.

THE TEN YEARS' WAR

In Cuba, the Spanish army's tyrannical rule continued through the years while the Civil War was raging across the water to the north. The next bid for the island's independence came in 1868. It was launched by a wealthy planter and attorney who lived in the southern province of Oriente. Perhaps inspired by the Civil War, he sought not only freedom for Cuba but also for its slaves.

His name was Carlos Manuel de Céspedes. On October 10 of that year, at the head of one hundred young Cuban friends and black slaves, he proclaimed a rebellion and demanded that the army's iron-fisted reign be ended, that Cuba's slaves be gradually emancipated over the next few years, and that the right to vote be awarded to everyone on the island (prior to the army rule, only a privileged few had been allowed to vote for the representatives being sent to the Spanish parliament; the vote had never been awarded to people born in Cuba who were regarded as inferior to the Spanish-born). The Céspedes proclamation unleashed a revolt that was to be fought mainly in Oriente and the provinces along Cuba's eastern coast. It was to go down in history as the Ten Years' War.

It was a war that saw Céspedes's followers form a republican government of their own in 1869 and name him as president. It was a war that brought revolutionaries flocking to his side from all parts of Cuba. By 1870, Céspedes had forty thousand men—Cubans and black slaves—under arms. It was a war of guerrilla fighting that took more than two hundred thousand Cuban and Spanish lives. It was a war that saw the rebels burn plantation fields and sugar mills, damage railroad lines, and destroy government installations. It was a war that saw the authorities capture and execute Céspedes. And it was a war that finally ended in February, 1878, when Spain sent a representative—Marshal Arsenio Martínez Campos—to meet with the rebel leaders.

From Campos, the rebel leaders received a number of promises. Cuba was to remain a Spanish state, but the people were to enjoy the civil rights that were granted to all under the Spanish constitution (a new democratic constitution that had been enacted in 1876) and were to be represented in the parliament at Madrid. The army's rule, which had been in effect since de Heredia's day, was to end. All the revolutionaries were to be "forgiven" and were to go unpunished. Although the island was still to have a Spanish governor, the people were to be in charge of their local affairs, handling them by means of elected provincial assemblies and town councils. The slaves who had fought on either side in the revolt were to be freed, with emancipation soon to come for all other slaves.

PROMISES KEPT, PROMISES BROKEN

The Spanish kept their word so far as the slaves were concerned. In an effort to make the revolution less appealing to the slaves, Spain had passed a law in 1870 that freed all slaves over the age of sixty. Now, as the 1880s dawned, a law took effect that called for the gradual abolition of slavery. In 1886, full abolition was granted, and in 1893, blacks were awarded equal civil status with whites.

But the Spanish failed to keep their word in other matters. Though saying that the revolutionaries were to be "forgiven," they now demanded that the Cubans pay for the damages done in the war. And, though saying that all were to enjoy the civil rights granted by the constitution of 1876, the Spanish refused to give the vote to anyone born in Cuba unless a fee of twenty-five pesos a year was paid for the privilege. The right to vote remained only with those who had been born in Spain. As a consequence, thousands of Cubans were kept from playing a part in the election of the provincial assemblies and town councils. Making matters even worse, the local Spanish officials began to choose the members of the assemblies and councils. Public anger at these actions—and at an economic depression that swept the island and left thousands jobless—mounted over the years. It finally reached such a pitch that the government in 1895 tried to subdue the people by suspending all the constitutional rights that had been granted.

Immediately, the leaders of the Ten Years' War took action. They summoned the people to arms and a new rebellion exploded throughout the island. There was fierce fighting everywhere, with the Spanish army controlling the cities and larger towns while the rebels commanded the rural areas and villages. The Spanish appointed a new governor, Valeriano Weyler. He treated the rebels savagely, setting up concentration camps and filling them with captured fighters and their supporters, all of whom were left to die of starvation and disease. The island's food supply was disrupted by the havoc. Havana and the area around it suffered a famine that claimed fifty-two thousand lives.

A CONCERNED UNITED STATES

In the United States, President William McKinley watched the rebellion with deep concern. The United States had long enjoyed a healthy trade with its neighbor. That trade was now especially important because, in the wake of the Ten Years' War, Cuba had become the United States' chief supplier of sugar. Further, American companies had invested heavily in the Cuban sugar industry. They had bought plantations and had constructed refineries. They had also invested in the mining of the island's mineral wealth. In all, the American investment in Cuba now totaled upwards of $50 million. It was an investment that was being endangered by the rebellion.

Deciding that he must act to protect the American sugar and mining interests in Cuba, McKinley urged Spain to release Cuba and let it become an independent nation. His plea angered the Spanish because it put them in a dangerous position at home. The Spanish knew that, if they let such a long-time possession go, they were sure to hurt the pride of their people—wound it so badly that the government might end up with *two* rebellions on its hands.

But the Spanish also knew that, if something were not done to end the Cuban conflict, McKinley might try to settle matters by sending American troops into the island. This would mean war with the United States. Already drained financially by the costs of fighting the revolutionaries, the Spanish had no desire for further trouble. And so they offered autonomy—independence while remaining within the empire—to Cuba.

It was a proposal that pleased McKinley. But it was flatly rejected by the Cuban rebels. They insisted that the island be completely freed and allowed to become an independent nation.

The proposal and its rejection triggered fresh outbreaks of violence in Cuba, especially in Havana. McKinley now took another step—one that the Spanish had feared. Although not actually sending troops into the island, he dispatched the cruiser *Maine* to the Bay of Havana. The president said that he was ordering the warship there "to protect the lives and property of U.S. citizens" in the city.

Soon after their arrival in early 1898, the *Maine* and its crew met with disaster. The United States was also plunged into war with Spain—and into years of agonizing political and military entanglement with Cuba.

3

WAR AND ENTANGLEMENT

The date was February 15, 1898. Night had fallen on Havana. Suddenly, the city was jolted by what seemed to be a deafening crash of thunder. People rushed into the streets. They saw a deep red glow above the harbor waters. Thick smoke rolled in over the docks.

It came from the *Maine*. An explosion had torn the cruiser wide open amidships as it rode at anchor out in the bay. The *Maine* sank quickly to the muddy bottom, taking 260 of its officers and men to their deaths.

In the years since that horrible night, no one has been able to say for certain why the ship exploded. Perhaps the cause had been internal—some lethal combination of electricity, coal gas, and gunpowder. Or perhaps there had been sabotage. Perhaps the Spanish, angry at America's intervention in their Cuban problem, had attached a submarine mine to the *Maine*'s hull. Or perhaps a band of Cuban revolutionaries, hoping that the United States would blame Spain for the disaster and go to war on the island's behalf, had planted the mine.

"REMEMBER THE *MAINE!*"

Only one thing can be said for certain. A wave of sorrow at the loss of so many young American lives rolled across the United States. The sorrow turned to outrage in the next days when a naval investigation could find no internal cause for the explosion. This left the terrible suspicion that the *Maine* had been sabotaged. Immediately, the United States public accused Spain of destroying the ship and demanded vengeance.

In their outrage, it is more than likely that the American people were putting the blame on an innocent party. Spain had no desire to do something that would bring on a war with the powerful United States. This was made clear when President McKinley had asked the Spanish to leave Cuba. Unable to depart for fear of triggering an uprising at home, Spain had tried to please McKinley by offering to make Cuba an autonomous state within its empire.

Why did Americans everywhere ignore this fact and demand vengeance on Spain? In great part, the blame lies with two newspaper tycoons of the day—William Randolph Hearst and Joseph Pulitzer. For several years, their newspapers in New York City—Hearst's *Journal* and Pulitzer's *World*—had been battling each other for subscribers and had been trying to win readers with sensational stories about Cuba in which the Spanish were usually depicted as villains. For example, in 1897, the *Journal* reported that Spanish officials had boarded an American passenger ship on its arrival at Havana and had arrested, stripped, and searched three young Cuban women. The story was later shown to be false.

The wreck of the battleship
Maine *in Havana harbor*

(Note: The sensational—and sometimes fictional—reporting produced by the Hearst-Pultizer war has gone down in the history of the press as "yellow journalism." The term comes from a comic strip, called "The Yellow Kid," that appeared in the Sunday editions of Pulitzer's *World*.)

With radio and television still in the distant future, the print press was the main source of information for the American people of the day. Its influence was as strong on the public of the late 1800s as television is on our lives today. Consequently, the sensational Hearst-Pulitzer reports had been sent across the country and had helped to create an anti-Spanish feeling nationwide. When disaster struck in Havana harbor, that feeling erupted into a frenzied demand for war—a demand that was heard from coast to coast in the cry, "Remember the *Maine*! To hell with Spain!"

Reacting to the outcry, President McKinley went before Congress on April 11, 1898, and said that the problem in Cuba had to be ended—by force, if necessary. Congress, as angry as the public, agreed and passed a resolution that sent the country to war against the Spanish. The resolution called for Spain to give up its authority in Cuba and withdraw its troops, and for the United States to send troops to the island and keep them there until peace had been restored. As soon as the Cubans formed a government of their own, the U. S. forces would leave.

The resolution was passed by Congress on April 19. Two days later—on April 21—the United States formally declared war on Spain.

THE SPANISH-AMERICAN WAR

Ranking as one of history's shortest conflicts, the Spanish-American War lasted less than four months. It was fought in Cuba and nearby Puerto Rico and in Spain's major possession in the Pacific Ocean, the Philippine Islands.

U.S. troops landing in Cuba in 1898

In Cuba, U.S. troops captured the city of Santiago and the area around it. When American forces landed at Puerto Rico, they met with almost no resistance. In the Philippines, a U. S. Navy force under Admiral George Dewey caught the Spanish fleet in Manila harbor and destroyed it, losing not a man in the process. He then blockaded the port until the arrival of the American troops that moved ashore and forced the surrender of the city.

The war, claiming only several hundred American lives (but resulting in several thousand Spanish fatalities), came to an end on August 13—a peace that was formally established on December 10, 1898. On that day, at the end of a series of meetings held in France between American and Spanish representatives, the Treaty of Paris was signed.

THE TREATY OF PARIS

The terms of the treaty were set down by President McKinley. Harsh and unyielding, the treaty made several demands that cost the Spanish dearly in territory. First, Cuba was to be granted its independence. Next, Spain was made to give Puerto Rico to the United States, plus the island of Guam in the Pacific. Finally, the Spanish were forced to sell the Philippine Islands to the United States for $20 million. The United States took Puerto Rico and the Philippines as a means of ridding the Caribbean and the far Pacific of Spanish influence; Guam was seen as a valuable supply and wireless station for the American navy.

Though Cuba was to be liberated from Spain and become an independent nation, it was not given full independence immediately. Rather, the treaty called for the island to be made a protectorate of the United States, meaning that it would be under American care and control. The United States, repeating a position stated in the congressional resolution of June 19, made it clear that the care and control would not be permanent. It would last only until peace and stability had returned to the war-torn island and the Cuban people had established a country of their own. The government in Washington, D.C., said that it had no intention of making Cuba into a U.S. possession.

And so the Cuban people were free—but, for the time being, in name only. Many of their number were angered by the new arrangement. They hated the idea of Cuba as a U.S. protectorate. Though their northern neighbor had helped them win their freedom, they had no love for the United States because they felt that American companies had long been exploiting the island's people by taking over so much of the sugar and mining industries. They also argued that Washington, contrary to McKinley's promises, would never relinquish its control of Cuba for fear of placing the U.S. sugar and tobacco investments in jeopardy. In all, as the Cubans saw matters, they were simply trading one ruler for another.

In these opinions, they were echoing the feelings of one of their great revolutionary leaders of the 1890s, the poet José Martí. Before his death in the battle of 1895, Martí had called for freedom from everyone, including the United States and its Cuban business involvement. He had long distrusted the United States because of that involvement.

A Spanish rule of some four hundred years ended for Cuba on January 1, 1899. The United States assumed control. The American Army's General Leonard Wood was named military governor of the island. His forces took over the reins of government. Those reins would remain in U.S. hands until May 20, 1902.

They were reins that Wood held firmly. The rebels had formed a government during the fighting, but he did not give it any power in those first days of peace. Rather, Wood allowed the rebels to do no more than hold a few civil offices. He had several reasons for acting as he did. For one, he knew that many of the rebels hated the idea of being a U.S. protectorate and might well work against him.

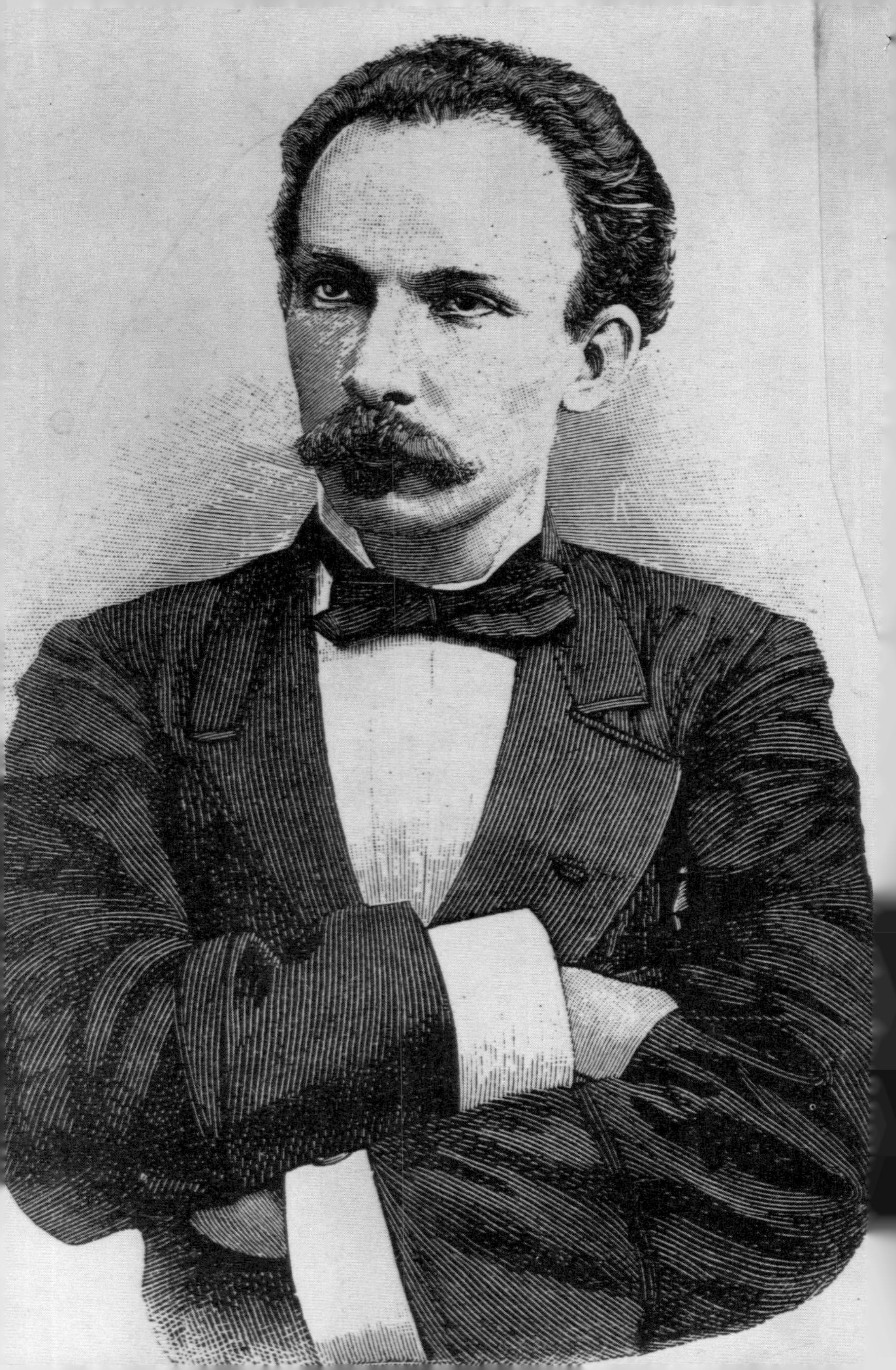

For another, the general felt that a firm control of the island until stability returned was necessary to protect the American sugar and mining investments there.

Above all else, Wood saw that the rebels, though they all shared the desire for national independence, were split into many small groups. Each had its own political ideas and aims. Not one of the groups was large enough to form a government that would truly represent the bulk of the Cuban people. Steps would need to be taken to establish a government that *did* represent the people. In the meantime, it was felt that there must be a strong U.S. hand to ensure that no one group assumed too much power.

But Wood and his men did much for the island while they were in charge. The army launched public works projects to improve Cuba's schools, its public administration facilities, and its sanitation system. The Army Corps of Engineers laid down highways and built a railroad line from Havana in the northwest to Santiago de Cuba in the southwest. Prior to the line's construction, travel between these two major cities had taken ten days. The time was now cut to twenty-four hours.

The U.S. army was also responsible for a campaign that freed Cuba of a terrible health hazard that had plagued it for years—yellow fever. An army medical team, headed by Dr. Walter Reed, worked with the Cuban scientist, Dr. Carlos Finlay, and established the truth of a theory

Cuba's great poet José Martí was killed in battle in 1895. The previous year he had been prevented by the U.S. government from leading a company of armed Cuban revolutionaries from the United States to Cuba.

that Finlay had long held—that the disease was spread by the bite of the *Aedes aegypti* mosquito. Once the theory was shown to be true, the job of eradicating the mosquito was handed to the sanitation troops of Colonel William Crawford Gorgas. Gorgas declared full-scale war on the mosquito and attacked it in its favorite breeding place— standing water. His men drained the swamps around Havana; poured away water that had gone stagnant in rain barrels. In places in which standing water could not be easily removed, they covered it with oil to suffocate the larvae. They installed window screens in homes and public buildings so that the mosquito could not work its way indoors to strike its victims.

The Gorgas war was a successful one. Within ninety days of the start of his campaign, the city of Havana was free of yellow fever cases for the first time in centuries. When the campaign was launched elsewhere in Cuba, yellow fever began to disappear from the entire island. Gorgas went on to win international fame by ridding the Isthmus of Panama of yellow fever. In earlier years, the disease had thwarted all efforts to build the Panama Canal. Gorgas's successful battle with the mosquito there (and his war against malaria at the same time) made possible the eventual construction of the canal. In time, Gorgas was named Surgeon General of the United States.

A CONSTITUTIONAL CONVENTION —AND TROUBLE

While the U.S. army was carrying out its various construction and health projects, there was activity on the political front, activity aimed at giving Cuba its eventual independence. Under General Wood's supervision, delegates were elected to a Cuban Constitutional Convention in September, 1900. There, they were to write a constitution for the new country, modeling it after the U.S. constitution.

On convening, they were surprised to find that the United States wanted several provisions attached to the new Cuban constitution. The United States had always promised that it would leave Cuba when stability was restored. But now it had come up with provisions saying that its control of the island would end only if certain conditions were met. The conditions had been developed by Secretary of War Elihu Root and had been approved by the U.S. Congress. Root called for such conditions as:

"Cuba should make no treaty that would impair her sovereignty . . . the United States might intervene for the preservation of Cuban independence or the maintenance of a government adequate for the protection of life, liberty, and the pursuit of property . . . and the United States might lease lands necessary for coaling or naval stations."

Though developed by Root, the conditions were contained in a document known as the Platt Amendment. This was because, needing to have them approved by Congress, Root had asked Republican Senator Orville Platt to present them in a bill for Senate approval. Platt had done so and had earned for himself a hated place in Cuban history.

The delegates, though willing to model their constitution on the U.S. constitution, were outraged by the Platt Amendment. They looked on it as being high-handed and were especially angered by the statement that "the United States might intervene for the preservation of Cuban independence." As they saw it, this gave the United States the right to send in troops and take control of the island on any pretext. Nor did the delegates like the idea that the United States might lease lands for naval and coaling stations. Such leases would give the American military a constant and intimidating presence in Cuba.

In total, the delegates felt that the Platt Amendment, if attached to their constitution, would not make Cuba an independent country at all. Rather, it would make the island little more than a protectorate of its northern neighbor. The old desire for annexation to the United States had long since passed in most Cubans. They wanted to be completely on their own.

For its part, the government in Washington, D.C., saw the Platt Amendment as a prudent measure. The view was that the Cubans were new at the job of living independently and that they were divided into various political groups, some of them hot-tempered and rash. There was every chance that the island might be torn apart by future uprisings. Further, there was always the chance that, as a young and small country, Cuba might one day become the prey of some land-grabbing European power. Faced with these possibilities, the United States felt that it needed the right to take protective action whenever its Cuban investments seemed threatened.

The Convention delegates were so upset by the amendment that they sent a committee to Washington to meet with Root and voice their fears. Root replied by saying that the Platt Amendment "does not diminish Cuban independence; it leaves Cuba independent and sovereign under its flag." He assured them that the United States had no wish to place Cuba under its thumb. "The United States will only come to its rescue in extreme cases to help Cuba preserve its absolute independence."

Root finished with: "God grant this extremity never be presented."

Despite Root's assurances, the Cubans remained suspicious of the amendment. Nevertheless, realizing that U.S. control would not end unless it was accepted, they appended the measure to the nation's new constitution. Under its provisions, the United States immediately leased the land for a number of military installations, among them the sprawling naval base at Guantánamo Bay, which lies along the island's southern coast. It is a base that the United States despite the unfriendly Castro government, continues to hold to this day. The Platt Amendment remained in effect until 1934 when a new treaty was negotiated with Cuba and all its provisions were dropped—except the American right to the Guantánamo base.

During the years that it was in force, the amendment—and the desire to protect American investments in Cuba—saw the United States continually entangled in the island's problems.

YEARS OF ENTANGLEMENT

With its constitution written and in place, Cuba elected its first congress in 1902. On May 5 of that year, the congress met for the first time. It took over the government from the U.S. military on May 20, with Cuba at last becoming an independent nation, a republic.

For the next three decades, the nation was headed by five presidents. They were, in turn, Tomás Estrada Palma, José Miguel Gómez, Mario García Menocal, Alfredo Zayas, and Gerardo Machado y Morales. Each man's term was marked by turmoil that reached out to touch the United States.

Tomás Estrada Palma

Palma held office from 1902 to 1906. During his tenure, Cuba enjoyed a healthy prosperity, chiefly because a trade treaty with the United States enabled more of the island's sugar to be shipped northward than ever before. But, despite this prosperity, Palma's term ended in personal disaster and a nationwide rebellion.

Palma himself has gone down in history as an honest man who was surrounded by corrupt officials. Pocketing public funds and exacting bribes from everyone who sought to do business with the government, these officials earned the enmity of the people and caused the public to lose confidence in Palma.

So much confidence was lost that Palma feared he would be defeated when he ran for reelection in 1906. His fears drove him to forget his honesty. He won reelection by "stuffing the ballot box"—that is, by padding the voter rolls with the names of nonexistent people and then having his henchmen use the names in casting ballots for him.

Word of what Palma had done reached the public and they greeted his victory with a rebellion. Insurrectionist troops surrounded the capital city of Havana. U.S. Marines rushed in from the Guantánamo base to keep order. Palma resigned. Cuba was left without leadership. The United States again assumed command and governed the island until 1909, when a presidential election was held and José Miguel Gómez took office.

José Miguel Gómez

Official corruption was again on view during the Gómez administration. In fact, it was said to reach new heights, with Gómez himself profiting from the bribery and the personal use of public funds. He was known throughout Cuba as Don Pepe Tiburón, meaning the "shark." And, of the many people who had dealings with the government, Gómez was suspected of favoring those who had supported the Spanish during the fight for independence.

Gómez showed himself as prejudiced against Cuba's black people, granting them only a few government offices. In an effort to better their fortunes, the blacks formed their own political party, the Independent Party of Color. Gómez replied by having his supporters in congress demand a law forbidding the formation of "movements composed of the same race or color."

The result was a bloody race war that erupted in 1912. It took the lives of thousands and caused the United States to dispatch Marine reinforcements for the protection of the Guantánamo base. Because of the outbreak, Gómez lost his bid for reelection in 1913. He was replaced by Mario García Menocal.

Mario García Menocal

Menocal's administration did much to help Cuba's economy. But corruption still played a part in the Cuban government—a corruption that saw the president fill numerous, high-paying government posts with his relatives. Then, when Menocal ran for reelection in 1916, he attempted to win through the use of violence, with his henchmen attacking opposition candidates and their supporters. These tactics brought on a brief revolt headed by former president Gómez. Menocal managed to fight off the uprising and was reelected.

U. S. President Woodrow Wilson helped to put an end to the uprising by announcing that the United States would not support any Cuban government that was established through revolutionary means. The United States was fast approaching its entry into World War I and Wilson did not want to be burdened with dealing with further upheavals in the island.

In 1917, Menocal joined the United States in declaring war on Germany. With the demand for sugar increasing during the war, Cuba enjoyed a booming prosperity in the months following. Sugar prices rose to a record level of 22.6 cents per pound and held near that level until 1920. Then, suddenly, an economic depression struck many parts of the world. The sugar market collapsed. The per-pound price dropped to $0.0325. Cuba faced a terrible economic crisis at the very time that its people replaced Menocal with a new president in 1921—Alfredo Zayas.

Alfredo Zayas

Zayas at first earned widespread respect by cooperating with the United States to better Cuba's financial condition. He obtained a loan of $50 million for financial and works projects from the United States. Because of the loan, the island's economy improved in the next two years.

But the loan caused trouble in some quarters. Many Cubans felt insulted when the United States, troubled by the corruption that had long been seen in the island's officials, insisted that an American—General Enoch Crowder—be placed in charge of distributing the $50 million. This requirement was seen as an intrusion into Cuba's affairs and caused a wave of anti-American sentiment.

Then, when Menocal had brought prosperity back to Cuba, his opponents accused his officials of the very same thing that had caused such insult when it had troubled the United States—corruption. Revolts broke out against Menocal and he became so unpopular that he lost his bid for reelection in 1924.

Onto the presidential stage now stepped Gerardo Machado y Morales. He became Cuba's first dictator, to be followed by yet another, Fulgencio Batista y Zaldívar. Their reigns bring us to the next chapter.

4

TWO DICTATORS

Gerardo Machado y Morales, a wealthy businessman, was elected president in 1924. He enjoyed widespread popularity during his first months in office because of a promised program of political reform—reform aimed greatly at reducing the corruption that had been seen for so long in Cuban government officials.

A DICTATOR EMERGES

The program failed to materialize, however, and Machado's popularity began to slip. The slip became a tumble when the people realized that his administration was as corrupt as those that had preceded it. Machado bribed politicians to do his bidding. He bullied opposition newspapers into silence. Most frightening of all, Machado revealed that he wanted to be a dictator who would rule for as long as possible. This came to light in 1927 when he bribed and threatened the Cuban congress into changing the constitution of 1901 so that his terms of office would be extended to six years. The original constitution had called for four-year presidential terms.

Machado was now widely hated. Nevertheless, he won his 1928 bid for a second term by running unopposed after bribing all the opposition parties not to put up candidates of their own.

As if life under Machado were not bad enough, the Cuban people were next struck with an economic disaster. It was triggered in 1930 by a tariff bill that the U.S. Congress enacted into law.

Cuba had prospered in the recent years not only because of the $50 million that it had received on loan from the United States. Cuba had also prospered from its sugar trade with the United States. But now, the new tariff law (called the Hawley-Smoot Act for its two congressional authors) placed high import duties (taxes) on a variety of products coming into the country, among them Cuban raw sugar. Instantly, American importers turned to less expensive sugar sources—to nontaxed supplies from the Philippines, Puerto Rico, and Hawaii.

And, instantly, there was economic chaos in Cuba. The price of the island's sugar plummeted. Warehouses became jammed to the rafters with sugar that could not be sold. Workers in the fields and refineries lost their jobs. The island's economy was reduced to shreds, with matters growing even worse when Cuba was caught in the great depression that spread across the world in the early 1930s.

Hungry and jobless, the Cuban people grew angrier with Machado because he seemed powerless to stop the tide of economic catastrophe. The public unrest developed into a minor rebellion in 1931. Machado smashed the rebellion with the Cuban army. Then, fully revealing himself to be the dictator that he had always been in his own mind, he unleashed a reign of terror to keep the population subdued. He turned his long-established secret police force loose to kill thousands of rebellious citizens. He proclaimed martial law and set the army to patrolling the cities and countryside. He abolished freedom of speech. He set up government machinery to censor the press. He denied everyone the right to assemble.

AN EMISSARY FROM PRESIDENT ROOSEVELT

With the island in such upheaval, thousands of Cubans fled to the United States. Their leaders sought help from the U.S. government. The United States was asked *not* to send in troops, but to exercise the provisions of the Platt Amendment by urging Machado to change his policies. Accordingly, President Franklin Roosevelt ordered a Caribbean expert with the State Department, Sumner Welles, to Havana as his personal emissary. His real job, however, was to mediate a peace between Machado and the anti-government groups.

Machado, now fearful of the widespread rebelliousness, cooperated with Welles. The president went so far as to restore to the Cuban people their constitutional rights to assemble, speak freely, and enjoy a free press. But his action was to no avail. The public hatred of Machado continued unabated.

A DICTATOR FALLS

The hatred was now running so deep that Machado's days were numbered. In August, 1933, the country's transport workers struck for better wages and were soon joined by other unions. Machado ordered the armed forces to break the strike, only to see some of his top military officers turn against him. The rebelling officers moved troops into Havana, trained the cannon at the city's Cananas Fortress on the Presidential Palace, and ordered Machado to resign his post. At first, he haughtily refused. But then he realized that the officers had gained control of most of the army.

They had the manpower and the weapons to dispose of him and his followers whenever they wished. Machado gave in and submitted his resignation in early August 1933.

Some days later, fearing for his life, Machado flew to Nassau in the Bahama Islands. He spent the rest of his days in exile.

With Machado's departure, representatives from some of Cuba's political parties met and named an interim president to lead the country until the people themselves could elect a president. Named to the post was Dr. Carlos Manuel de Céspedes, the grandson of the wealthy planter who had triggered the Ten Years' War back in 1868. Céspedes immediately took several positive steps. He dropped the constitutional amendments that had been made for Machado in 1927, restored the constitution of 1901, returned to the people their civil rights, and promised them a presidential election in the near future.

But, despite these steps, Céspedes found himself on troubled ground. Cuba's economy remained in ruins. Various groups were calling for drastic political and social changes. For instance, the nation's communist organizations wanted to see a soldier-worker government. Besides all this, there were groups who, either seeking personal power or sincerely hoping to aid the stricken country, wanted to overthrow Céspedes and take charge themselves. A band of Havana students and young military officers were secretly plotting such an action, as was a group of older officers. And so were six army sergeants. Their leader was the man who, in time, would become Cuba's next dictator.

SIX SERGEANTS AND A NEW PRESIDENT

On the night of September 4, 1933, little more than three weeks after Céspedes had taken office, a group of six sergeants walked into the headquarters building at Camp Columbia, a sprawling army installation located just outside Havana. Leading them was a small but stockily built man with a mane of thick and coarse black hair. The son of a laboring family, he had a mixture of Spanish, Indian, black, and Chinese blood in his veins. His name was Fulgencio Batista y Zaldívar.

Unholstering his pistol, Batista made his way to the office of the army chief of staff. He entered, pointed the gun at the officer behind the desk, told him that the sergeants were taking over the army, placed the army officer under arrest, and then sat down at the desk as the army's new commander.

From that moment on, the events of the night took on a dizzying pace. Batista's men strode through the camp's living quarters and, at gunpoint, ordered all the officers to leave the installation. Batista himself telephoned army bases throughout the island. Only sergeants and other enlisted men were on duty at the bases because their officers had retired for the night. When they were told that Batista was taking command of the army and was going to form a new government for Cuba, they all agreed to follow his leadership. They then called their officers and flatly told them not to report for duty in the morning because their jobs were to be filled by others.

By morning, with the backing of all the sergeants and a few officers who came over to his side, Batista had the entire army in his hands.

Batista was thirty-two years old when he staged his bloodless takeover. An ambitious man, he had been orphaned at the age of thirteen and had held a variety of jobs—among them tailor's apprentice, grocery clerk, and sugar plantation foreman—before joining the National Army in 1921 as a stenographer. During his twelve years in the service, Batista had proven himself an expert stenographer and a hard worker. Praised by his superior officers for his competence, he had risen to the rank of sergeant. But he had been powerless to advance to officer status. His laboring background gave him no family connections with officials high in the government. For promotion to the officer ranks, one needed a "helping hand" from people of influence.

Ambitious as he was, highly intelligent, and interested in politics, Batista was not only frustrated at being unable to achieve officer status but also angry at the political and economic chaos in Cuba. And so he had decided to take matters into his own hands. When he did so, the sergeant, as the old saying goes, "killed two birds with one stone." First, he abruptly entered the officer ranks, appointing himself a colonel. Second, as the army's new commander, he was in charge of the country's single most powerful force. With its nine thousand armed men behind him, no one could stop him from forming a new government.

Batista, however, had no desire to become Cuba's president. He planned instead to operate behind the scenes as the army's chief. And so he placed the reins of government with a commission of five respected public figures. At their head was a university professor, Dr. Ramón Grau San Martín. On Batista's instructions, the commission replaced President Céspedes with Grau San Martín. The idea of a presidential election at some future date was forgotten.

ACTION AND ANGER

On taking office, Grau San Martín quickly angered several countries, among them the United States. In an effort to strengthen the Cuban economy, he announced plans to suspend repaying the money that the island had borrowed

Cuba's strongman,
Fulgencio Batista y Zaldívar

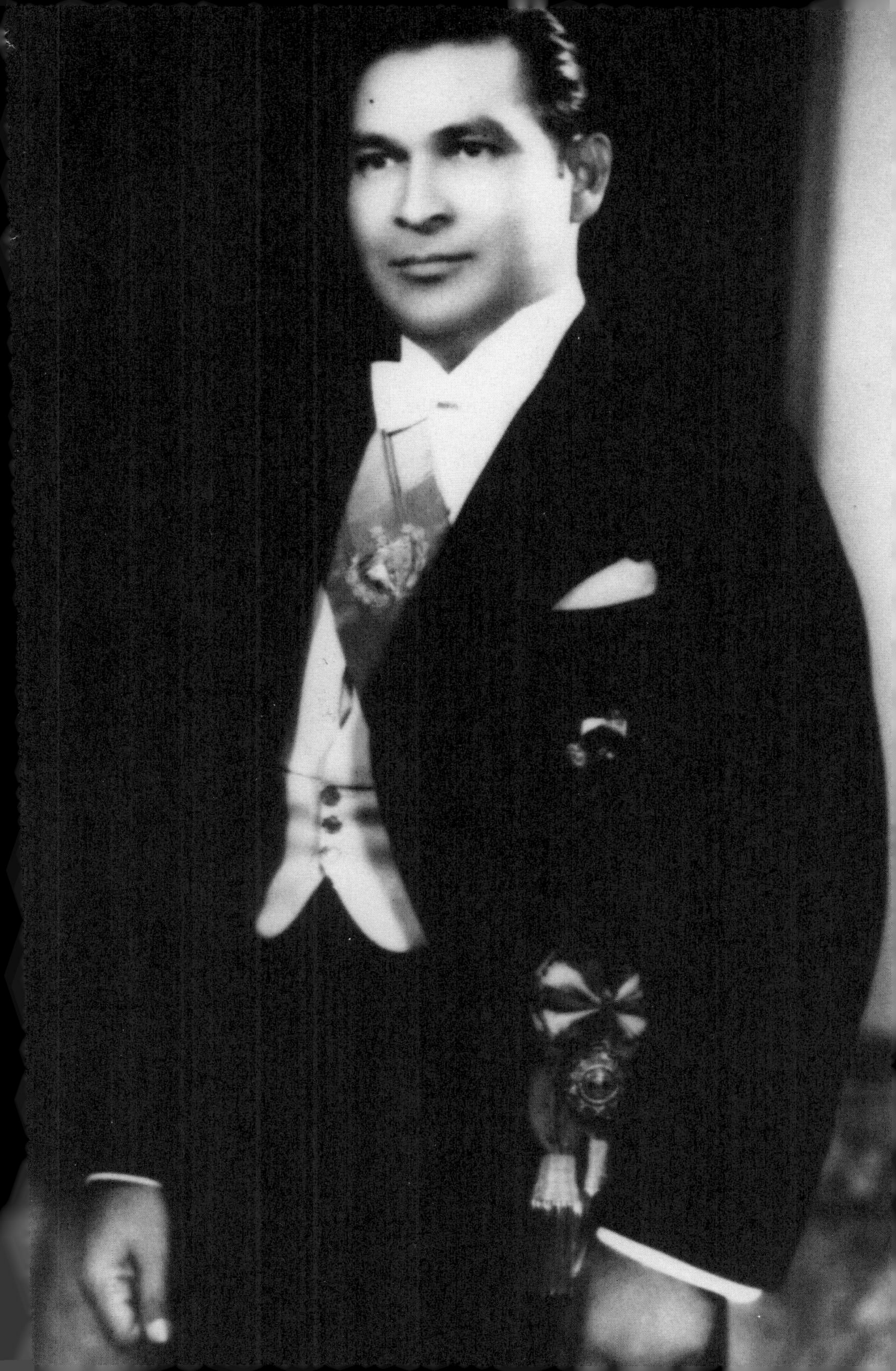

over the years from foreign nations. Then he tried to force the electric power companies to reduce the rates they were charging to their customers. Like Cuba's sugar operations, the power companies were owned in great part by U.S. firms. At the time, their rates were among the highest charged anywhere in the world. But, as exorbitant as the rates were, the power companies refused to lower them. Grau San Martín responded by taking control of the power plants on January 14, 1934.

U.S. reaction was immediate. Knowing the army commander to be the most powerful figure in the island, the American ambassador, Jefferson Caffrey, went to Batista and told him that the United States would never cooperate with a government headed by Grau San Martín. Batista understood full well what this meant. Until a president friendly to its northern neighbor was installed, the financially troubled Cuba could expect no further U.S. loans. Batista met with Grau San Martín and urged him to resign. The result: Grau San Martín stepped down. Batista ordered that he be replaced with Carlos Mendieta. Grau San Martín had been in office a mere four months.

MENDIETA AND BATISTA

Mendieta, with the all-powerful Batista working behind the scenes, was to last for two years. They were years that brought Cuba a mixture of happy and unhappy experiences.

On the happy side, the nation's economy improved somewhat. The improvement came when the United States reduced the high tariffs that the Hawley-Smoot Act of 1930 had imposed on Cuban sugar. Sugar began to move northward from the island in increasing amounts.

Further, in 1934, the Cuban government negotiated a treaty with Washington that dropped the hated Platt Amendment from the constitution of 1901. At last, the island could feel completely independent, free of the threat of U.S. intervention in its affairs. Under the terms of the treaty, however, one provision in the amendment remained. The United States was allowed to continue leasing the naval base at Guantánamo Bay.

On the unhappy side, Mendieta and Batista ran the government with a dictatorial hand. A presidential election was never mentioned. The government restricted the voice of the press. Though the economy was improving, the times were still far from good and a number of unions struck for better wages; Mendieta and Batista had the army put down the strikes—brutally—and then dissolved the unions. There was widespread corruption among government officials. Inconsistent economic policies halted the improving sugar market, caused widespread unemployment, and brought the government near bankruptcy.

Again, public discontent spread through the island and brought the danger of rebellion. And, again, America's Sumner Welles stepped in. He urged Batista to avoid havoc by giving the people the right to elect their president. Batista, knowing how unpopular his association with Mendieta had become, agreed. Cubans went to the polls in January 1936—for the first time since 1928—and elected as their president Miguel Mariano Gómez, the son of one-time President José Miguel Gómez.

The country may have voted a new leader into office, but everyone knew that Cuba's true leader was still Batista. This became crystal clear late in 1936 when Gómez opposed a Batista plan to create a number of new schools to be directed by the army. Gómez saw this as a Batista effort to increase the power of the army—and, therefore, Batista's personal power—over students who would one day be voters. Batista replied to Gómez's opposition by having congress remove him from office.

Gómez was replaced by Vice-President Federico Laredo Brú. Brú served until the autumn of 1940.

BATISTA'S GROWING POWER

In those years, Batista—now known throughout the country as "Cuba's strong man" and "the maker and breaker of presidents"—strengthened his already awesome power. He did so by increasing the size of the army from nine thousand to twenty thousand troops and by developing them into fine soldiers through a highly disciplined training program. Most people did not object to this growing power because Batista also performed a number of works that pleased them.

For one, realizing the country's great need for increased educational opportunities, the people did not object when Batista established the series of military-staffed schools that Gómez had opposed—thirteen hundred in all. And the people certainly did not object when he ordered the construction of such needed facilities as hospitals, tuberculosis sanitariums, and orphanages. Further, Batista had public support when he attempted to establish cooperative agricultural projects to benefit the country's farmers and urged social security for workers and farmers.

But, despite these works, Batista eventually became unpopular with a growing number of people. Their discontent centered on the government graft that enriched Batista and his friends and on the brutal ways in which he intimidated and silenced his opponents. Once again, Cuba was becoming ripe for upheaval.

To avoid trouble, Batista changed his ways in the late 1930s. He spoke of becoming more democratic in his outlook. He brushed aside many of his colleagues known for their bribery and pocketing of public money. He called for the dissolution of the *Falange*, Cuba's fascist party (a party that believed in rule by force) and legalized the long outlawed but widely popular Communist party. Then, in February 1940, he resigned with the rank of major general from command of the army.

(Note: Batista returned to uniform within weeks. Without his firm leadership, a number of politically ambitious officers tried to lead the army in a revolt against the government. Batista quickly reasserted control and suppressed the uprising.)

PRESIDENT BATISTA

The year 1940 also saw Batista take two other steps in keeping with his changed outlook. He gave his approval to a new constitution being considered by the Cuban congress; the constitution was adopted and remained in effect for more than three decades (Cuba today operates under a constitution adopted in 1976). Then, once the constitution was approved, Batista demanded that one of its main provisions be immediately honored. He called for the scheduling of a general election to choose a new president.

When the election was held in July 1940, Batista's name was on the ballot. At last coming out from behind the scenes, he defeated his opponent—Dr. Grau San Martín—by a decisive margin.

Batista took office for a four-year term in October 1940. It proved to be a successful term. Helped by American loans, Batista launched a series of public works projects, among them the construction of hospitals throughout rural Cuba. He guided through congress a minimum wage law that increased salaries for workers in both private industry and the government.

The constitution of 1940 was similar to its predecessor of 1901, except in certain details. One difference required a president not to seek election for eight years after completing his four-year term. Consequently, Batista was unable to stand for reelection in 1944. He left Cuba on a tour of Central and South America, after which he settled at Daytona Beach, Florida, where he spent much time playing tennis, long one of his favorite sports.

In 1948, Batista returned to Cuba and won election to the congress as a senator from Santa Clara province. He began to organize his own political party, called Unitary Action, and announced that he would be a candidate for president in the June 1952 elections.

But he did not wait for the election. Claiming—truthfully—that the nation was in chaos and the people furious because of unbridled government graft, Batista led a group of young army officers to Camp Columbia at dawn on March 11, 1952. There, as he had done nearly twenty years earlier, he seized control of the military. Before noon, he occupied the Presidential Palace and took the reins of government. By then, the deposed president, Carlos Prío Socarrás, had fled the country.

Batista then assumed dictatorial powers, saying that he was doing so for the purpose of restoring order to the country. He suspended constitutional guarantees for forty-five days. He increased the pay of the police and army to ensure their loyalty. He canceled the June elections, but promised to hold them at a later date.

At that moment in 1952, Batista's grip on Cuba seemed stronger than ever. But it was a grip that would soon be broken by a young attorney who was evolving into a rebel leader. His name was Fidel Castro.

5

A NEW REVOLT, A NEW LEADER

Batista's government stood on shaky ground for several months. The Cuban people were shocked and unsettled by his sudden takeover. Foreign countries were reluctant to do business with a nation in turmoil. Matters soon improved, however. Batista overcame the foreign doubts and brought in new trade and investments from the United States and elsewhere. The economy began to improve.

But there was no improvement in Cuba's political life. Batista proved to be the same dictator that he had been in the 1930s. He took control of the country's press and radio. He suppressed his opponents. Forgetting about the promised presidential election, he began to rule Cuba with an iron fist.

As a result, the island found itself heading toward a fresh revolution. A new rebel movement began to take shape in secret. By the spring of 1953, there were rumors that a major revolt was brewing to unseat Batista. And there was the widespread belief that its chief financial backer was the president whom Batista had toppled—Carlos Prío Socarrás. Prío was a millionaire who had made much of his money through graft and gun-running. He would never forgive Batista for overthrowing him.

THE REVOLT OF JULY TWENTY-SIXTH

On July 26, 1953, the expected trouble became a reality. Some two hundred young men attacked the Moncada Barracks, an army installation in Oriente Province. The attack was accompanied by scattered uprisings throughout the island. Everything ended in failure, with Batista's forces quickly suppressing the revolutionaries.

But the revolt could not be considered a complete failure. It achieved one major result. It produced the determined and charismatic revolutionary leader who would, in time, drive Batista from power and change the direction of Cuban history. That new leader was Fidel Castro.

FIDEL CASTRO

Nicknamed "Ruz," Castro was a twenty-six-year-old attorney from a prosperous family. He had been a source of trouble for Batista ever since the dictator's 1952 takeover. At that time, Castro had filed a lawsuit with the Court of Constitutional Guarantees in Havana. The suit charged Batista with violating the Cuban Civil Code in his takeover and with illegally holding the various offices he had taken for himself—those of President, Prime Minister, Senator, Major General, and Civil and Military Chief. In all, Castro demanded that Batista be stripped of his offices and punished for crimes against the Cuban constitution.

Perhaps in Batista's pay—or perhaps frightened of him—the majority of the court rejected Castro's lawsuit. It ruled that the 1952 takeover had been legal on the vague grounds that "revolution is the font of law." Frustrated in a legal effort to move against Batista, Castro began making plans for a revolution to oust the dictator. With friends, he organized a rebel force of young idealists, dedicated, as he claimed, to Cuba's 1940 constitution and to the democracy and the social justice it promised.

Dark-haired, brown-eyed, deep-chested, and standing 6 feet 3 inches (191 cm) tall, Castro was a vigorous man who was no stranger to revolutionary movements. While a law student at the University of Havana, he had served as president of a militant group, the University Students' Federation. In 1947, he took time out from his studies to participate in an unsuccessful attempt to overthrow Generalissimo Rafael Trujillo, dictator of the Dominican Republic.

Now, in 1953, Castro led the attack on Moncada Barracks, only to see many of his fighters die. He and his fellow survivors were immediately jailed. About thirty of their number were freed a short time later. The remainder—including Castro and his brother Raúl—were made to stand trial.

Because he was a lawyer, Castro was allowed to conduct his own defense. During the trial, he gave a speech that was to become one of the most significant addresses in Cuban history. Speaking without any notes whatsoever as he faced the court, Castro presented an outline of Cuban history, citing its economic and social conditions and its governmental repressions. He quoted such thinkers as Thomas Aquinas and Thomas Paine on the right of revolution, and others on the need to depose tyrants. He then outlined his own program for revolutionary change.

Though eloquent and impressive, the speech did not save Castro. He and brother Raúl were sentenced to fifteen years in prison. Once behind bars, Castro reconstructed the speech. He smuggled it out a few sentences at a time in letters to friends. The sentences made their way past the prison censor because they were invisible—written in lime juice between the lines of the letters—and came into view only when held over a flame. When all the sentences were painstakingly pieced together, the speech was published in pamphlet form under the title *La Historia Me Absolvera*—meaning in English, *History Will Absolve Me*.

The title was taken from the final lines in the speech: "I do not fear the fury of the wretched tyrant who snuffed out the lives of seventy brothers of mine. Condemn me. It does not matter. History will absolve me."

In pamphlet form, the speech became known as the Gettysburg Address of the Cuban Revolution. Over the next years, it drew countless of the island's people to Castro's cause.

A NEW DEVELOPMENT

In 1955, Batista had the Cuban congress grant an amnesty to the island's political prisoners, among them Fidel and Raúl Castro. It was an act that opened prison gates everywhere (the term *amnesty* means "an official forgetting of past troubles and offenses"). With it, Batista hoped to gain two ends. He hoped to quiet the nation's rebels and their many supporters. And he hoped to convince the Cuban public and the world at large that he was not really the tyrant that his enemies had painted him to be.

When granting the prisoners amnesty, Batista tried to appear as if he were not afraid of their opposition. He was releasing them, he said, so that they could "become normal human beings . . . do something useful for society . . . and confine their political opposition to channels prescribed by law." But there is no doubt that Batista was nervous about Castro. Because the rebel attorney had such a formidable gift of oratory, Castro was forbidden to speak on the radio.

Once released, Castro tried to conduct his opposition to the Batista regime in a nonviolent manner. But, unable to reach a mass audience because he was forbidden the use of the radio, Castro left Cuba and settled in Mexico.

While in Mexico, Castro organized Cuban exiles into a revolutionary army dedicated to liberating their homeland. Christened "the 26th of July Movement" in memory of the Moncada attack, it was a tiny band that finally numbered just over eighty men. But, despite its small size, the unit troubled the Mexican officials, who had no wish to see their country's relations with the Cuban government ruptured. They took steps to hamper the unit's development. On one occasion, the Mexican officials arrested Castro for training men to invade a friendly nation. On another, they raided his camp, confiscated some weapons and ammunition, and informed Batista of what was going on there.

But their actions were to no avail. Castro's army survived the harassment, attracting not only Cubans but also revolutionary spirits from throughout Latin America. Among the arrivals was a man who became internationally known as one of Castro's top aides—Ernesto "Ché" Guevara de la Serna.

Interested in Latin American leftist movements since young manhood, Guevara was a communist doctor from an upper-class Argentine family. In 1954, he went to Guatemala and was appointed a medical officer in that country's armed forces. When a revolution overthrew the Guatemalan government a few months later, Guevara fled to Mexico and soon thereafter joined Castro's movement. He worked with Castro for years, always with loyalty and dedication.

(Note: When Castro won control of Cuba in 1959, Guevara served as the nation's minister of finance and as the president of the Cuban national bank. In 1966, Guevara traveled to Bolivia to direct a guerrilla movement there. He was captured by a Bolivian army unit and executed.)

Guevara was not the only man who was important to Castro as the revolutionary army took shape. Help also came from former president Prío Socarrás, who was still smarting over the humiliation of being deposed by Batista. He gave Castro $100,000 to help arm, feed, and clothe the troops. The two men were political opposites and had no liking for each other. Prío was a millionaire, a capitalist, and a man with a taste for enriching himself on government graft. Castro, though born of a prosperous family, was a radical, an opponent of government by and for the rich, and an opponent of capitalism. Yet Prío offered the money and Castro took it because both were united in their hatred for Batista.

ATTACK

At the time he formed his army, Castro made public a promise. He told the press: "In 1956, we will be free or we will be martyrs."

Now, on November 25, 1956, he made ready to keep that promise. With his eighty-two armed fighters, Castro boarded the decrepit yacht *Granma* and sailed for Cuba. He was headed for a landing spot some miles to the west of the city of Santiago.

His plan called for the cooperation of a three-hundred-man army that was headed in Cuba by a young revolutionary named Frank Pais. The Pais army was to start things by taking control of Santiago with a series of guerrilla attacks. Then, when Castro came ashore, he and Pais would join forces. They would move northward to the town of Manzanilla and engage Batista's army. In the meantime, other Castro supporters were to launch uprisings in various parts of the country.

It was a strategy that was doomed to failure. Pais and his troops did their part and controlled Santiago for several hours. But the uprisings that were to erupt throughout the country failed to materialize. And the Castro unit ran into trouble. The ocean between Mexico and Cuba proved rough and the men quickly became seasick. Then high winds drove the *Granma* off course, with the result that the men came ashore behind time and in the wrong place—in a swamp rather than on a firm beach.

For three hours, Castro and his bedraggled revolutionaries sloshed through mud and water up to their waists. When they finally reached firm ground, they found Batista's army in place and waiting for them. There was the metallic rattle of gunfire. Within minutes, all but a dozen of the ill-fated party were either dead or in captivity.

Batista sent out a triumphant announcement to the nation. Castro had been killed.

IN THE SIERRA MAESTRA

The announcement was a falsehood. Castro was very much alive. With his brother Raúl, Che Guevara, and nine other fighters, Castro had escaped from the coast. He was now deep in the wilderness of the Sierra Maestra.

Located north of Santiago, the Sierra Maestra is a mountain area of some 1,500 square miles (3,885 sq km). It has a population of approximately fifty thousand. Most of its people are *guajiros*—"peasants"—who make their living by harvesting the sugar cane, tobacco, and coffee that grow wild all about them.

At the time Castro entered the Sierra Maestra it was one of the most primitive regions in the country. There were no communications systems, no schools, no hospitals, no doctors, and no government officials. For years, the Batista government had ignored the area's people, abandoning them to disease and starvation. Their only contact with the government came when they met an occasional army patrol on one of the mountain trails. The army patrols were feared and hated. They robbed, raped, and murdered the peasants.

It was in this wild region that Castro, mustering his strength after the terrible defeat outside Santiago, began to rebuild the 26th of July Movement. He found that he had come to just the right spot for the job because he received help from the mountain people.

Actually, he won that help. His studies had shown Castro that revolutionary armies always draw their greatest strength from the support of the people. He set about gaining that support here in the mountains. He treated the *guajiros* with fairness and kindness. His men paid for all the local food they ate. Ché Guevara put his skills as a physician to work, caring for ill or injured peasants whenever he could. Castro made certain that, whenever army patrols came searching for him, he and his fighters stayed well away from the villages so that the peasants would not be endangered. He established a firm policy of executing landowners who informed the army of peasants who gave assistance to his men.

All these factors paid handsome dividends for the rebel leader. The mountain people gave him their wholehearted support. They spied for him. They hid his men—now called the *Fidelistas*—from the army patrols. They tended his men wounded in skirmishes with the patrols. Many joined his force and showed themselves to be superb fighters.

THE MOVEMENT GROWS

While Castro was regrouping in the Sierra Maestra, the Batista government was busy. Knowing that Castro was there, the dictator increased the number of army patrols in the area. At the same time, Batista had the government-

Two symbols of the revolution are shown here. At the top, a rebel sights down the barrel of a grenade launcher during a skirmish in Oriente Province with government troops. In the bottom photo, Fidel Castro holds his gun in readiness while his revolutionary flag flies in the background.

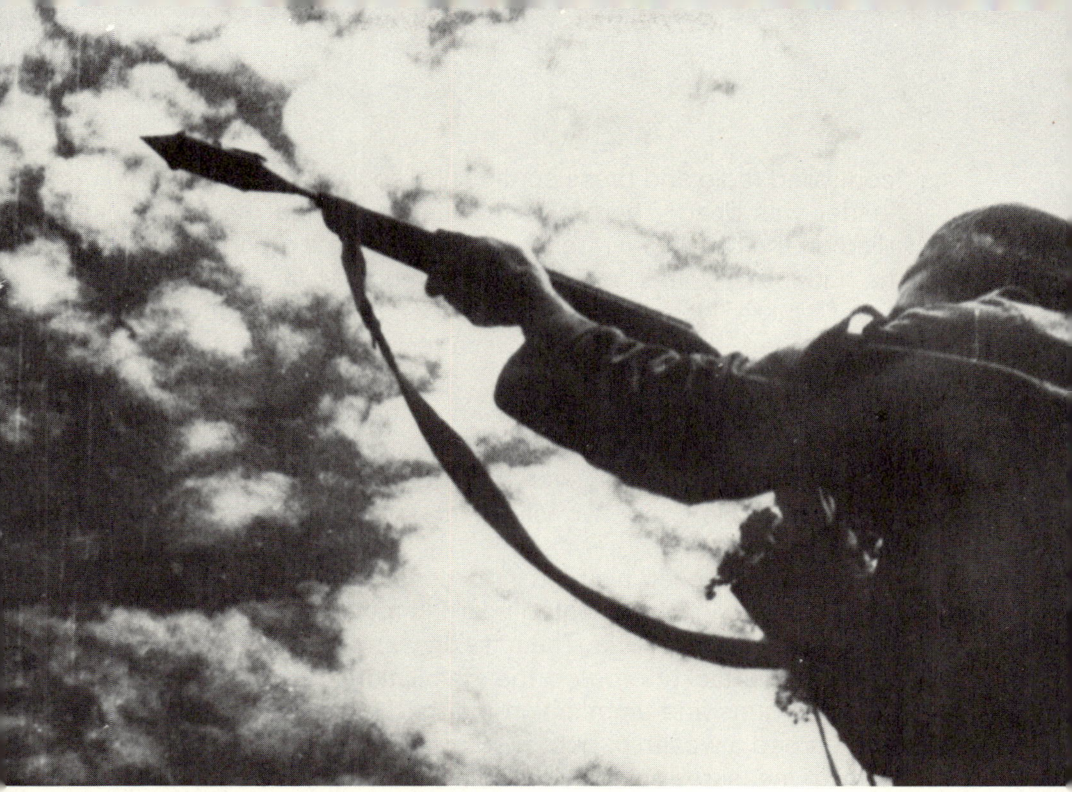

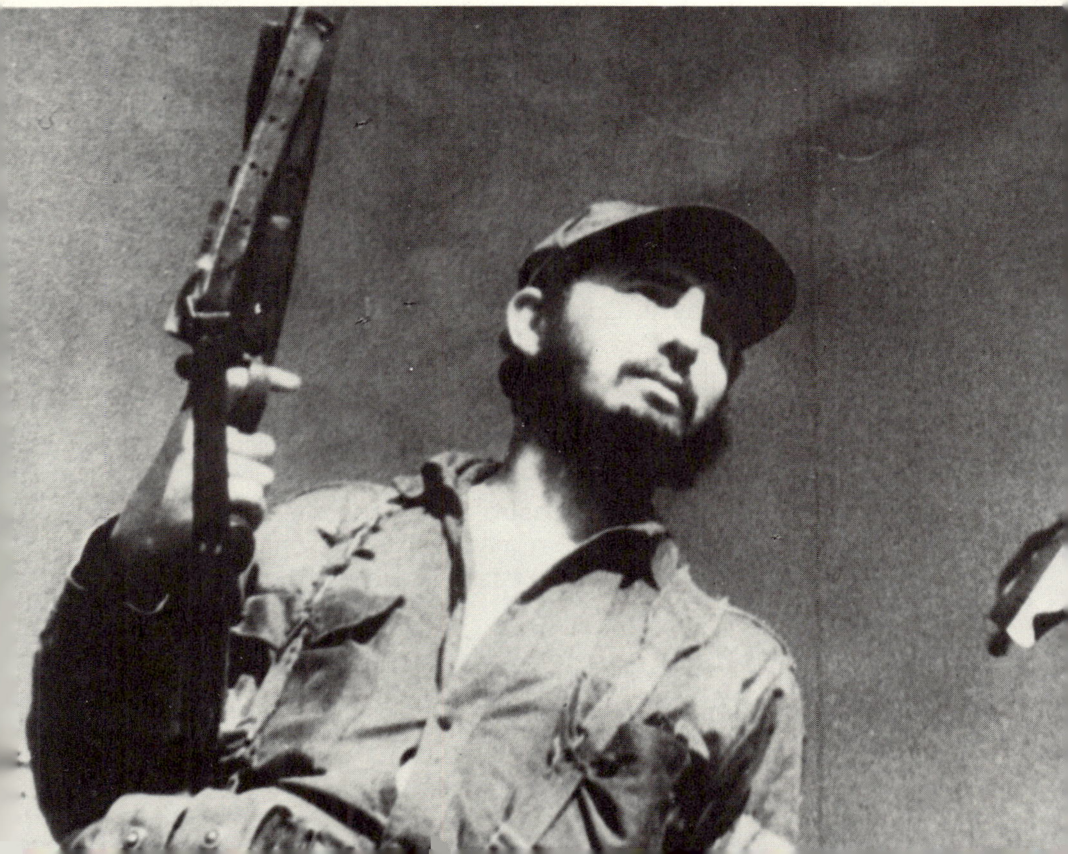

controlled radio and press continually report that the rebel leader was dead. There was that first claim that he had died on the beach near Santiago. Then came a report that he had lost his life in a skirmish at a mountain army post. Later, there were stories that rebel bodies—Castro's among them—had been found scattered along trails after skirmishes.

Castro heard the reports. He knew that to gain support for his cause he must prove that he was alive and that he was as determined as ever to further the 26th of July Movement. He took two steps to supply the needed proof.

To begin, he led his men in an assault on the La Plata army post, which was located near the mouth of the Sierra Maestra's La Plata River. The mission was a complete success. The attackers routed the installation's troops, took over the guns and ammunition that had been left behind, and earned a wealth of publicity. Even Batista's strict censorship measures could not keep the word from spreading through Cuba that Castro was alive and had scored a great victory.

Next, Castro smuggled a foreign newsman into the Sierra Maestra for an interview. That newsman was Herbert Matthews. On February 17, 1957, he talked with and photographed the bearded leader, after which a series of articles friendly to Castro appeared in the *New York Times*. The Matthews articles were widely read in the United States and elsewhere, with word of what they had to say making their way to Cuba. Written by a neutral outsider, they removed any last doubts that Castro was alive. Quite as important, they caught the imagination of the people of Cuba and abroad and helped to further Castro's movement by picturing him as a folk hero who personified the hopes of the common man.

Matthews described Castro as an educated man of great ideals and courage, a man with a personality that was overpowering, a man of fanatical dedication to his movement, and a man with great powers of leadership. As for the movement itself, Matthews described it as socialistic and nationalistic.

Socialistic refers to various economic and political theories that advocate collective or governmental ownership of a nation's production and goods. *Nationalistic* stems from *nationalism*, which means a loyalty and devotion of such a degree to one's country that the interests of that country are placed above those of all other nations. The two terms were to attract a growing number of Cubans to Castro over the years. To many, the first promised them a greater share of their country's wealth. And, to many, the second meant a break from the United States and its longtime hold on the Cuban economy.

Matthews also made a point that was of particular interest to many Americans. There was the fear in the United States that, with his socialistic and anticapitalistic views, Castro might be a Communist. Matthews reported Castro as saying that Cuba's Communists had nothing to do with the 26th of July Movement.

The Matthews article was followed by many other interviews in the next months. Journalists from all over the world trooped into Castro's Sierra Maestra camp. Chewing on his ever-present cigar and with the words literally pouring out of him, Castro always proved to be, in newspaper jargon, "good copy." He told the reporters that he wanted only to free the Cuban people; that his movement was not connected with political groups of any sort; and that, without such a connection, it was free of the exploitative type of politics that had long governed not only Cuba but also many other nations. Since he had nothing to do with other political groups, he insisted that he was not a Communist.

(Note: Occasionally, someone who professed to know Castro well would contradict him and claim that, indeed, he was a dedicated Communist. Castro always denied these charges.)

When they were published, some of the interviews were favorable to Castro, and some were not. But, regardless of their content, they all achieved one result. As Castro had hoped, they had left no doubt that he was alive and in action. And they had turned Castro into one of the world's most famous men of the late 1950s.

The rebel leader was not only world famous but he was also stronger than ever. His 26th of July Movement was attracting a steady stream of revolutionaries from throughout Cuba. His army had grown in size until it now numbered several hundred men.

The time had come for the next step in his campaign to overthrow Batista.

6
TOTAL WAR— AND VICTORY

Castro took that step on April 1, 1958, little more than a year after the tragedy of his invasion attempt. He proclaimed "total war" on the Batista regime. It was to be a total guerrilla war.

Immediately, Castro stepped up his attacks on the army patrols in the Sierra Maestra. Hitherto, his men had struck at the patrols on a few occasions. Now, they hit them regularly, attacking and then, in guerrilla fashion, fading back into the underbrush. Beyond the Sierra Maestra, his men sabotaged a number of high-tension transformers outside Havana, blowing them up with dynamite and cutting off the city's electrical power for fifty hours.

In other actions, roving guerrilla units began attacking buses and trains in various parts of the island; the assaults were intended to discourage visits by foreign vacationers and thus damage Cuba's tourist trade, a vital part of the country's economy; the tactic succeeded. Schools were bombed at night, bringing the island's public education system almost to a halt. Government facilities were also bombed—or set afire.

A vital part of Castro's war was a propaganda campaign. He set up a radio transmitter in his mountain stronghold and began a series of nightly broadcasts from what he called "the territory of free Cuba in the Sierra Maestra." He acquired a printing press that churned out pamphlets and leaflets for distribution throughout Cuba. All of Castro's radio broadcasts and printed material carried messages concerning his belief in a free Cuba and his hopes for a better future for all the people—or, to use his words, *his* people.

A HARVEST OF DISASTER

Gathering momentum as the months of 1958 passed, Castro's total war reaped a harvest of disaster for Batista.

First, each new month saw more and more Cubans drawn to Castro. His greatest support at this time came from the nation's poor, the ones who had suffered the greatest deprivation at the hands of the government. Thus, the revolutionary movement spread initially from the Sierra Maestra to the nation's other rural regions. Then it moved into the slums of the big cities.

It must be said that Batista was still widely tolerated among the nation's working and middle classes. Despite the corruption in the government, Cuba's economy was in good health and these people had no desire to jeopardize their livelihoods by rising against the dictator. Batista was heavily supported by wealthy landowners, industrialists, and business leaders. They all profited from the healthy economy. Many also either profited from the government corruption or were too influential to be troubled by Batista's dictatorial ways.

But there could be no doubt that Castro's growing strength was beginning to cost the dictator the support of some very important Cubans. In mid-1958, for instance, the leaders of the nation's labor unions declared themselves neutral in the Castro-Batista battle. So did the leaders of Cuba's major religious body, the Catholic Church.

Cubans everywhere understood what these declarations of neutrality meant. Someone was going to win and it might not be Batista. For the good of their followers, the union and religious leaders were readying themselves to be on working terms with whoever emerged as the victor. This understanding did nothing but damage Batista's prestige. (Later, the Catholic Church, in an effort to end the strife and bloodshed, would urge the dictator to resign from the government, a request that he would ignore.)

Batista's prestige was further damaged when the Cuban people learned that his soldiers were terrified of Castro. This fact was driven home in early 1958 when the news broke of what some soldiers had done on learning that their rural post was about to be attacked by a rebel band. They had set the place ablaze and had taken flight. Adjusting its target, the assault force had then decided to advance on a nearby town, where a large army contingent was housed—only to face troops so frightened that they offered but a token resistance before fleeing and leaving behind a wealth of arms and ammunition.

Worse, in May of the year, Batista threw a full-scale attack against Castro's Sierra Maestra stronghold. After suffering several defeats, the rebels drove the dictator's troops back out of the area.

Then, worse still, Batista suffered an unexpected reversal at the hands of his neighbor across the water to the north.

THE AMERICAN ACTION

No longer able to intervene in Cuban upheavals because the Platt Amendment had been canceled, the United States for a time took a neutral position in the Castro-Batista struggle, endorsing neither side. However, the

United States seemed anything but neutral because, as had been the case for years, its munition makers were selling arms to Batista—arms that he promptly used against Castro. Further, although President Dwight D. Eisenhower had no liking for Batista, the United States was maintaining friendly relations with the dictator to protect the American companies that had heavy investments in the island.

But now that look of friendliness suddenly disappeared. Disturbed by the growing turmoil and afraid that the revolution would end in a nationwide bloodbath, the United States placed an embargo on the delivery of all arms and munitions to the Batista government. Even orders that had already been paid for were canceled.

It was an action that did not cripple Batista because he could still obtain arms from other sources, among them Great Britain and the Dominican Republic. But it was a terrible slap in the face for the dictator, even though the United States went on insisting that it was neutral in the island's struggle. It indicated to the Cuban people that one of the world's biggest countries thought that Batista would soon fall and was preparing to be on friendly terms with the government that replaced him.

TROUBLE FOR CASTRO

Batista, however, was not alone in meeting disaster. Castro also suffered a major defeat. It came in early April, 1958—just eight days after he had declared total war on his dictator enemy.

On launching his total war, Castro issued a written declaration to the Cuban people. Containing twenty-two points, it outlined the kind of government that Castro was promising to establish at the time of his ultimate victory. Two of the points, however, required immediate action by the people. One called for a general strike, whereas the other urged all Cubans to stop paying their taxes. Both measures were aimed at helping to bring the Batista regime crashing down by crippling the economy.

It was the call for a general strike—a strike by all the nation's workers—that ended in Castro's humiliation. Scheduled for April 9, the walkout was too hastily organized and did not have the full support of the nation's workers. The result was a complete failure.

It was a failure that came about with blinding speed. The strike lasted but a mere two hours. In that time, everything seemed to go wrong. With the economic times being as good as they were, many workers refused to risk their wages by participating. And many of those willing to take the risk never learned at what hour they were to leave their jobs. The police had heard rumors of the coming trouble and were waiting with guns and clubs for the strikers. Members of the Cuban Communist party, who were dedicated to taking over the country for themselves rather than assisting Castro, sabotaged the strike by rushing to the defense of Havana's television station when a band of his student supporters tried to seize it so that they could broadcast the word of the walkout to the nation.

In itself, the failure was bad enough. But worse was yet to come. Batista moved savagely against those thought to be behind the strike. Within twenty-four hours after the collapse of the strike, some two hundred suspects had been apprehended and executed by the police. Many were gunned down by firing squads. And many were tortured to death.

The debacle was a grievous blow to Castro's movement—and a personal humiliation to him because, in his impatience, he had allowed the strike to take place with insufficient preparation. But it proved to be a temporary setback. Castro intensified his guerrilla attacks and bombings. His followers spread the message of his determination to give Cuba to the Cubans; he would topple a hated dictator; he would establish a government that allowed every citizen to share in the nation's wealth; and he would break the grip that outsiders, especially the Americans, had long held on the island's industry. That message, along with the press interviews that were depicting him as a charismatic leader, steadily won Castro increasing support. It was support that now came not only from the poor but also more and more from people of all walks of Cuban life.

A STRANGE INCIDENT

The revolution was beginning to snowball. Castro's army was beginning to number not in the hundreds but in the thousands. And Batista was beginning to suffer his series of disasters, chief among them the arms embargo imposed by the United States.

That embargo led to a strange incident in mid-1958. A rebel group headed by Castro's brother Raúl captured a Batista document that indicated that the United States was to deliver three hundred rockets to Batista via the Guantánamo Naval Base. Raúl, thinking that the United States had violated its arms embargo, retaliated by hijacking a bus from the base and taking its passengers—twenty-eight U.S. sailors and Marines—prisoner. Raúl Castro and his men then kidnapped nineteen employees of firms in which the United States had a financial interest—two sugar-refinery managers, twelve technicians with the Moa Bay Mining Company, two executives with the Nicaro Nickel Company, and three officials with the United Fruit Company.

Raúl informed the Guantánamo base of what his men had done. When the story made headlines all across the world, the rebels were surprised at the American rage it triggered. They meant to do their prisoners no harm and had intended only to voice an objection to the breaking of the arms embargo. But the Americans reacted as if the hostages were in danger of death. President Eisenhower told the press that he was sending a representative—Park

Wolham, a U.S. consular officer at Havana—into the Sierra Maestra to confer with Castro and "get live Americans back."

The matter stopped there. On hearing of Raúl's action, Castro ordered the immediate release of the captives. Helicopters from Guantánamo flew in and evacuated them. Apparently, the captives had been well treated during their stay with the rebels. Almost all of them returned with stories of the consideration, courtesy, and concern that had been shown them.

(Note: As matters turned out, the entire incident had occurred because of a mistaken reading of the captured document. The rockets did not constitute a breach of the arms embargo. The document referred to rockets that had been sent to Batista *before* the embargo went into effect.)

A REGIME COLLAPSES

By late 1958, the Castro movement was in full flower, with Batista about to suffer a final humiliation. That humiliation came in November when Cuba held its presidential elections. Batista, after taking control of the country in 1952, had given himself a democratic look by standing for election in 1954—an election he had won by intimidation. Now, in 1958, again trying to appear the democratic leader, Batista said that he would not stand for reelection because he was prohibited from doing so by the constitution. He gave his support to Andrés Riva Aguero.

The voters all knew that Batista "owned" Aguero and that the election would be a fraud. When the election was over, the dictator would still be in control of the country. Out of anger and fear—a fear engendered when both Batista and the Castro forces threatened harm to anyone who voted "the wrong way"—the people turned the election into a farce by staying away from the polls. In Santiago, 98 percent of the voters failed to appear, while 75 per-

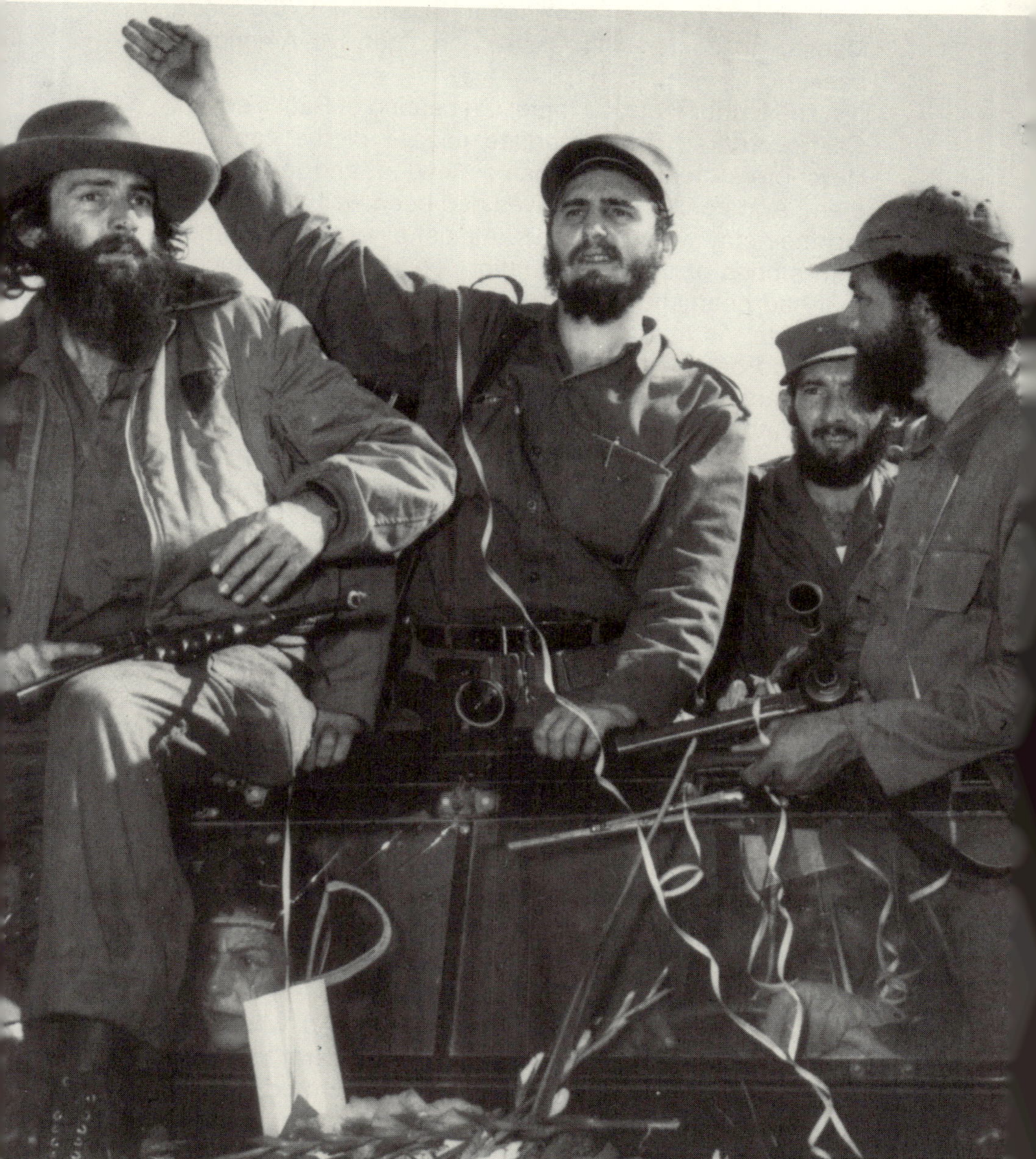

cent abstained in Havana. Aguero came away the winner in a one-sided victory.

Batista remained in power. But it was a power that was fast becoming meaningless. Months earlier, after the army had tried its full-scale attack on Castro's Sierra Maestra stronghold and had been repulsed, the rebels had come down from the mountains and had begun to fight their way northward. At first, they had taken a province at a time, but now, with their number estimated at fifty thousand men, they were sweeping up the length of the island. They were just a few weeks—perhaps even a few days—away from Havana.

The United States, still maintaining its neutrality in the upheaval, had hoped that the November voting would see a freely elected president take office. When that failed to happen, Washington urged Cuba to stop the fighting by installing a caretaker government and holding new elections.

The request came to nothing. By December 31, Castro's forces were fast approaching Havana. Batista realized the end was at hand. At 2:10 A.M. on January 1, 1959, the dictator and his family—along with his top military and civil officials—fled the country. Three air force planes flew the party to exile in dictator Rafael Trujillo's Dominican Republic. Before departing, Batista released a message to the nation. He said that he was departing to avoid further bloodshed.

In the next days, Castro's forces marched triumphantly into Havana. Castro himself arrived there on January 8, 1959. He was no longer simply a rebel leader. He was now the nation's leader.

Castro waves to the cheering crowd on his arrival in Havana on January 8, 1959.

TROUBLED NEIGHBORS

7

FROM SUSPICIONS TO MISSILES

Just before launching his total war, Castro had issued a written declaration to the Cuban people. It had contained twenty-two points. For the most part, these points had been Castro's promises of what he would do for the country when final victory was at hand.

Now, on entering Havana, the revolutionary leader began to keep those promises. Castro took the following steps: He established a provisional—temporary—government to serve until a general election could be held to choose the nation's representatives. The respected jurist Dr. Manuel Urrutia was named president of the provisional government. José Miro Cardona, long a Castro supporter, was appointed temporary premier (prime minister). This executive position was established in the 1940 Cuban constitution. The president and premier were to administer the government in cooperation with a committee of revolutionary leaders and known as the Council of Ministers.

Castro stated that his army would play no part in the government but would give it support. He named himself as the army's commander-in-chief. In taking this post, he was indicating that he did not plan to become a dictator but intended to leave the running of the government to others—to those chosen by the ballot. However, Castro kept the job for only a few weeks. In February, 1959, he and Premier Cardona became involved in a dispute over governmental policies. Cardona resigned and Castro took his place, with the command of the army going to brother Raúl. Castro has served as premier ever since.

He announced four basic government plans: (1) a civil service program was to be installed to ensure that government workers were hired on the basis of merit and not through bribery or the influence of highly placed friends or relatives; (2) the nation's land was to be redistributed so that it was placed in the hands of the many rather than the wealthy and privileged few; (3) Cuba's educational system was to be broadened and improved so that the nation's widespread illiteracy would be ended; and (4) Cuba's industrialization was to be accelerated to provide more jobs and bring greater wealth to the country.

THE UNITED STATES WATCHES

The promises were happily greeted by Cubans everywhere—except the wealthy who stood to see their riches or their land jeopardized because of them. The promises likewise pleased the United States.

Although it had adopted a neutral policy in the Castro-Batista struggle, Washington had watched Castro with worry. The United States had long been committed to frustrating the spread of communism anywhere in the world. There was fear that Castro, with his socialistic and anticapitalistic views, was a Communist. If so, he would be bringing a hated ideaology to within 90 miles (145 km) of America's front door. This fear was deeply felt despite Castro's repeated declarations that he had nothing to do with communism.

But, now, official Washington looked at his promises and found that they did not seem to be communistic in nature. Nor did they seem threatening to the U.S. industrial interests in Cuba. Castro gave no real indication that he planned to take these interests over and have them run by the government. Washington felt that such an indication would have certainly come from a Communist.

In light of these conclusions, the United States officially recognized the new Cuban government and its temporary president, Dr. Urrutia. Official recognition meant that Washington and the new Cuban government could have diplomatic dealings with each other.

TROUBLE ERUPTS

The two countries seemed to be getting off to a fresh and healthy start. But, almost immediately, trouble erupted between them. It was trouble that, in various forms, was to grow through the years and continue to the present, making Cuba and the United States into the troubled neighbors that they are today. In 1959 alone, it was marked by two major developments.

1. Into Havana Harbor

This trouble began when Batista fled and Castro's troops were entering Havana. Three U.S. Navy destroyers and two submarine tenders appeared in the harbor. Their mission was to protect and, if necessary, evacuate the Americans caught in a city that was being torn apart by unruly mobs bent on destroying anything that represented the Batista regime.

It was a legitimate precaution, but it was one that angered the Castro forces. American ships had never appeared during the Batista years. Their appearance now seemed to say that the United States was dropping its neutrality in the Castro-Batista struggle and was planning to interfere with the coming new government, just as it had interfered in Cuban affairs long ago under the hated Platt Amendment.

2. Problems for U.S. Companies

Though Castro had not said anything about taking over U.S. companies in the island, he began to move early in that direction, much to the consternation of their owners and Washington.

In March 1959, Castro ordered the U.S.-owned Cuban Electric Company to reduce its price rates in Cuba's rural areas. At the same time, he placed the Cuban Telephone Company—also U.S.-owned—under government management. He told the system's owners that they would be permitted to draw profits from their investment, but they would play no part in the company's management. The management duties would be handled by Cubans. Then Castro expanded the electric distribution system, especially in the rural areas, and reduced its charges.

Next, in May, Castro had the Council of Ministers adopt the Agrarian Farm Law. Aimed at distributing Cuba's land to more of the people, the law established limits on the amounts of property that individuals and business enterprises could hold. It also stipulated that foreign companies could go on owning Cuban land, *but only if such ownership proved to be in Cuba's interest.*

As U.S. owners saw it, this made them helpless victims at Castro's hands. They felt that it gave Castro the right to grab their land at any time he saw fit and for whatever reason he chose to give. A disturbed President Eisenhower demanded of Castro that there be "prompt, adequate, and effective" payment for any American-owned land the Cuban government might take.

CASTRO A COMMUNIST?

These problems were accompanied by yet another in 1959—the growing U.S. suspicion that Castro was a Communist. It was a suspicion that took on credence in July of that year when Castro flew into a rage on hearing President Urrutia publicly condemn the island's Communists. In a series of angry steps, Castro forced Urrutia to resign and then had the Council of Ministers appoint Osvaldo Dorticós as president. Dorticós was a former leader in the Cuban Communist party.

Adding fuel to the U.S. suspicions were the charges of many Batista supporters who had escaped Cuba and had exiled themselves to the United States. On their arrival, they told stories of how Castro was becoming a dictator, of how he was giving increasing power to the island's Communists, and how he—like the dictators before him—was using brutal means to silence his opponents. Castro accused the exiles of being political criminals who were trying to blacken his name. The United States, though understanding that they were Batista supporters, nevertheless gave the exiles sanctuary and, as we will soon see, began to use some of their number in a secret attempt to overthrow the new Cuban government.

An American diplomat spoke out in support of what the exiles had to say. He was Earl T. Smith, who had been ambassador to Cuba during the Castro-Batista struggle and who had deplored the Batista dictatorship. Smith said that, ever since the failed general strike that had opened Castro's "total war," the revolutionary leader had increasingly accepted the help and cooperation of his nation's Communists.

As the U.S. suspicions heightened, Castro continued to deny any Communist ties. During a 1959 visit to the United States, he told a meeting of reporters at the National Press Club in Washington, D.C.: "We are against all kinds of dictatorships. That is why we are against Communism."

But, so far as official Washington was concerned, his actions belied his words. Although the Cuban government, after years of strife, was in desperate need of money, Castro refused to seek a loan from the United States. Rather, he turned to the Soviet Union. At first, he did not try for a loan there. Rather, in February 1960, he and the Soviet government signed an agreement under which Cuba would receive Russian crude oil in exchange for the island's sugar. Soon, however, Castro was accepting Soviet loans—plus arms and military specialists. The Soviet specialists instructed Castro's army in the use of arms and began establishing military and missile bases on the island. In time, the Soviets were exerting as much influence on the Cuban government and economy as the United States had once done.

In July 1960, Castro began to work with yet another Communist nation. He signed a trade treaty with mainland China.

Finally, late in the year, Castro declared Cuba a socialist (his word for "Communist") country and established himself as head of state. He brought under government control some 382 major business enterprises and banks, including more than $1 billion worth of American-owned properties. He paid the United States no compensation for most of the American-owned properties. Then, at the end of 1961, Castro openly admitted what had become a certainty in U.S. minds. He announced that he was, and would be "until the end of my life," a Marxist-Leninist—in a word, a Communist. Then, in 1962, he helped to form what is today's Communist party in Cuba (it replaced the nation's earlier Communist party) and was named its leader, its first secretary.

OPEN HOSTILITY

By the time Castro admitted he was a Communist, relations between Cuba and the United States had deteriorated to open hostility.

Much of the hostility centered about the Cuban exiles who had settled in Florida. Many of their number were intent on doing to Castro what he had done to Batista. They were out to overthrow him. Their campaign opened when a few ex-Cuban military pilots obtained some old aircraft and flew single-plane raids on Havana—raids that showered the city with anti-Castro leaflets. Castro angrily claimed that Washington was financing these progaganda attacks because it thought him a Communist and did not want his government in the Western Hemisphere.

At one point, he attempted to buy arms from U.S. manufacturers for the purpose of repulsing the raids and defending Cuba against potential aggressors. Washington refused to allow the arms purchase and urged Great Britain to do likewise should the Cuban dictator approach any British munitions firms.

The United States contended that Castro would not use the arms to defend himself but to equip Communist revolutionaries who were planning to take power in other Latin American countries. Castro charged that, in reality, the United States was trying to keep his government weak so that it would be vulnerable to attack from within or without.

One of the worst moments for the two countries came in the latter half of 1960. At that time, Castro ordered the island's U.S.-owned oil refineries to process the crude oil arriving from Russia in exchange for sugar. The refineries refused to obey. Castro immediately took over the installations and placed them under government control. In retaliation, an angry Washington slapped a partial embargo on the U.S. import of Cuban sugar, a move that severely wounded the island's economy.

The latter half of that year produced a second bad moment. In September, Castro traveled to New York City to address the General Assembly of the United Nations. His speech was highly critical of the United States' actions toward Cuba. Afterward, he held a friendly meeting with another visiting foreign dignitary—Premier Nikita Khrushchev of the Soviet Union.

Then Castro returned home to close the year on a sour note. He gave a particularly anti-American speech in which he demanded that the staff of the U.S. embassy at Havana be reduced to eleven people. The demand was meaningless and was simply meant to be insulting. On January 3, 1961, President Eisenhower, angered by the insult and all the events of the past months, severed diplomatic relations with Cuba. As we will see in chapter nine, those relations have remained almost completely severed to the present day.

Matters between the two neighbors had reached their lowest point. Or had they? Worse was yet to come. The future was to bring two angry American-Cuban confrontations—in 1961 and 1962. The first would end in embarrassment for the United States. The second would bring the United States and the Soviet Union to the brink of war.

INVASION:
THE BAY OF PIGS

By the middle of 1960, the first Cuban exiles had been joined in Florida by others. The new arrivals were not necessarily Batista supporters, but were people from various walks of life—shopkeepers, doctors, teachers, artisans, laborers—who had found life under the new government intolerable.

(Note: More than 1 million Cubans would eventually leave their homeland and take up residence in the United States, with the great majority settling in Florida and adding much to that state's cultural and ethnic richness. This figure does not include the children born to the newcomers after they arrived in the United States. For a time, the Castro government seemed glad to be rid of the exiles and did nothing to halt their departure. Later, when Cuban-American relations became so strained that air service between the two countries was canceled, the refugees smuggled themselves into the United States aboard rafts, sailboats, and small fishing boats. In 1980, Castro angered the American government by emptying Cuba's prisons and mental institutions and sending the inmates north with the other refugees in what became known worldwide as the Mariel boat lift, so called because all the people departed from the Cuban coastal town of Mariel. Some 125,000 mental patients and prison inmates landed in the United States and have been a source of controversy ever since. Many found jobs and have lived successful lives. But many others ran into nothing but trouble. The New York police reported that, between 1980 and 1984, more than seven thousand Cubans were arrested in the city for various crimes. Between late 1980 and 1983, the Miami police charged some three thousand Cubans with just upwards of fourteen thousand misdemeanors, felonies, and criminal traffic violations. Many U.S. authorities have long believed that among the mental patients and prison inmates were agents sent by Castro to weaken the American spirit through drug peddling.)

The newcomers of the 1960s and 70s brought with them two kinds of stories. On the one hand, there were stories of how Castro was keeping the many promises he had made to the Cuban people. He had, for example, lowered all rents on the island by 50 percent, had passed a law making greater Social Security payments available to workers, and had established a committee to plan Cuba's economic development.

But, on the other hand, there were reports of how Castro had forgotten about the promised presidential election. He and his supporters held total power. The economy was bad and growing worse because the new government was inexperienced in financial matters and was mismanaging things. There was increasing discontent in the island. Revolutionary groups were forming. Castro might well one day face at some new leader's hands the very same fate that Batista had suffered at Castro's hands.

The U. S. government was by now convinced that

Cuba had become a Communist state. To stop the spread of communism in the Western Hemisphere, the island's government had to be toppled. On hearing the stories of unrest in the island, Washington decided that the time was ripe for an attempt to invade Cuba and unseat Castro.

The Central Intelligence Agency (CIA), assisted by certain officers in the Pentagon, was put in charge of plotting the attempt. The agency developed a plan for an invasion in which the United States would seem to play no part so that it could not be accused of illegally endangering the sovereignty of an established foreign government. The assault would be carried out by Cuban exiles who would be seen as making an effort to liberate their country. In secret, they would be trained and equipped by the CIA.

Some thirteen hundred exiles received their training at CIA bases in Guatemala. Castro picked up rumors of what was in the wind. He condemned the United States for dropping the attitude of neutrality it had long professed in regard to Cuba and accused Washington of planning the worst sort of intervention in the island's affairs. He alerted his defense forces and ordered them to be ready for an attack.

The attack came on April 7, 1961. Five ancient boats carried the thirteen hundred exiles from Guatemala and Nicaragua and deposited them at a point near the Bay of Pigs on Cuba's western coast. They were accompanied by old, unmarked American B-26 bombers that dropped leaflets urging the Cuban people to rise against Castro and join the attack force. The invaders expected that the leaflets would bring the island's dissidents to the Bay with assistance that would help to hold off Castro's army for seventy-two hours.

In that time, the attackers would set up a provisional government and appeal for help from the United States. On receiving the request, the United States would recognize the new government and could then legally intervene in the upheaval and complete the plan to unseat Castro.

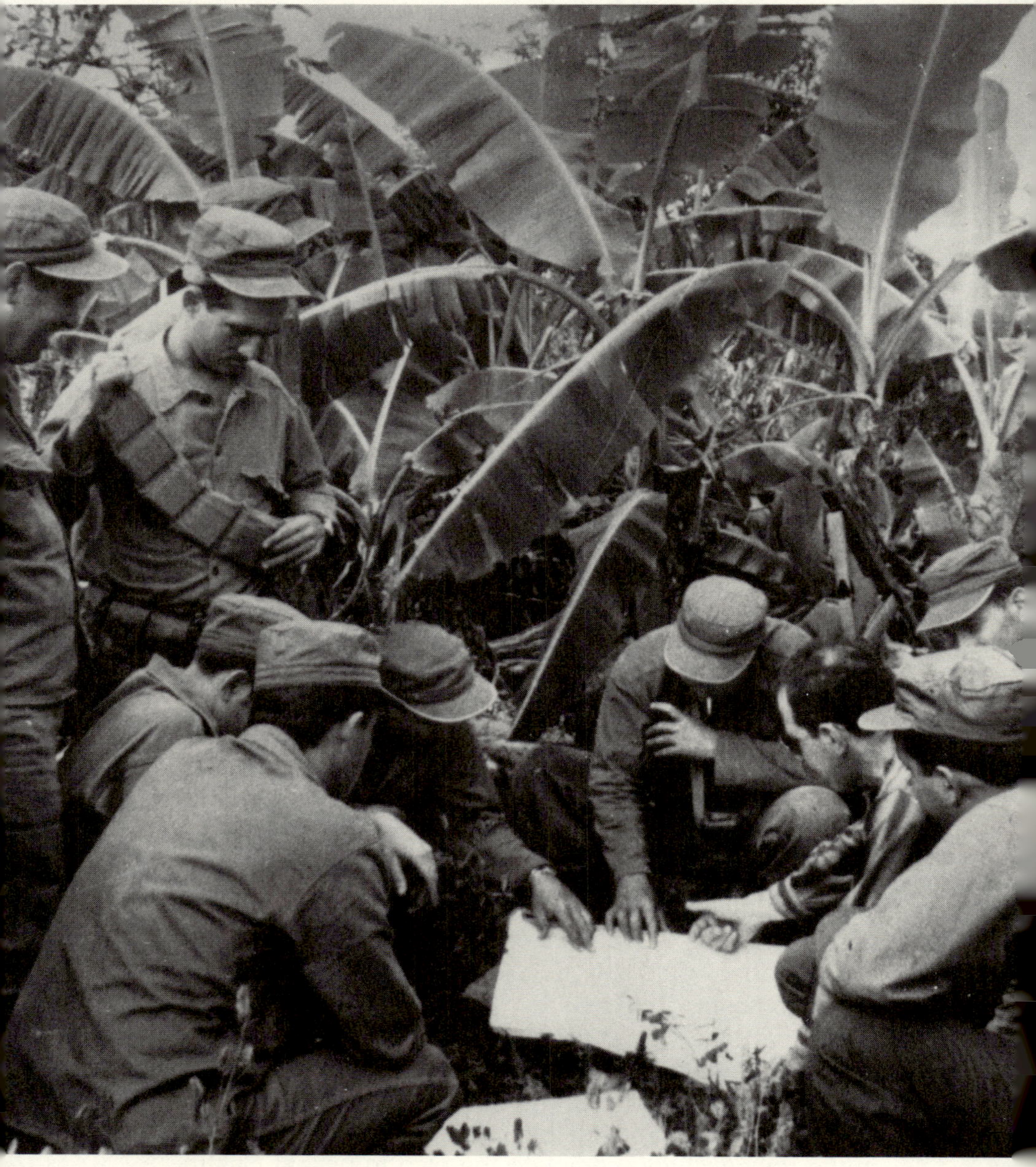

Washington had prepared for the request by placing an aircraft carrier and additional forces nearby. The personnel at the Guantánamo Bay naval base had also been increased.

But everything ended just as Castro's invasion from Mexico had ended back in November of 1956—in total failure. The expected assistance did not come from the island's dissidents. On being hit by Castro's air force, the attackers asked that U.S. Navy jets be sent to help them. The planes, however, never appeared. Within forty-eight hours, Castro's army and air force had soundly defeated the invaders, killing 150 of their number. The survivors escaped through a swamp and made their way into the mountains, only to be captured a short time later. Close to twelve hundred of the invaders were taken prisoner.

The Navy jets never arrived because President John F. Kennedy refused to permit their use. Additionally, he refused to allow the B-26 bombers to fly an attack mission after they had dropped their leaflets. He never explained his reasons for these decisions. It is suspected, however, that the president, knowing Cuba to be backed by the Soviet Union, felt that strong U.S. participation would threaten a war with Russia. Further, the invasion plan had been hatched during the Eisenhower administration and Kennedy had never liked the idea, presumably because he thought it had every chance of failing. He nevertheless allowed the invasion to take place and now, despite his opposition to the whole affair, he accepted full responsibility for its failure because he was in office at the time it was staged.

Anti-Castro forces training in Guatemala for the Bay of Pigs invasion

The American people were shocked at the news of the failed invasion. Many expressed anger at Washington for plotting an attack that they found as sneaky as Japan's assault on Pearl Harbor in 1941. Others were humiliated at the idea that a great nation had been unable to make the invasion succeed. Opinion varied on President Kennedy's decision concerning the B-26s and Navy jets. Some people lauded him for a decision that likely avoided a war with Russia. Others accused him of betraying thirteen hundred men who were carrying out an American plan.

Although the president's decision was widely supported by the American public, his prestige suffered a severe blow. He was to regain that lost prestige in little more than a year later—in the tension-filled month of October 1962.

THE MISSILES OF OCTOBER

In 1962, disturbing reports began to reach Washington from newly arrived Cuban exiles and other sources. The reports held that thousands of Russian soldiers were being transported to Cuba and that Soviet bombers and intermediate-range missiles were being based there. It was a well-known fact that Castro's involvement with the Soviet Union had deepened in the past months and that Russia was exerting an increasing influence on the island's affairs. To Washington, the current reports meant but one thing: the Soviet Union was strengthening the position of communism in the Western Hemisphere, right at America's doorstep. Something had to be done to stop the Soviet move.

The United States immediately set out to check the authenticity of the reports. Military planes equipped with cameras flew missions high over Cuba in an effort to locate the Russian army camps and missile bases. At first, the missions failed to bring back any evidence of a military

The port of Mariel, Cuba, two weeks after President John Kennedy announced that the Soviet Union had erected missile bases in Cuba. This U.S. Air Force photograph shows missiles being reloaded on Soviet ships for removal.

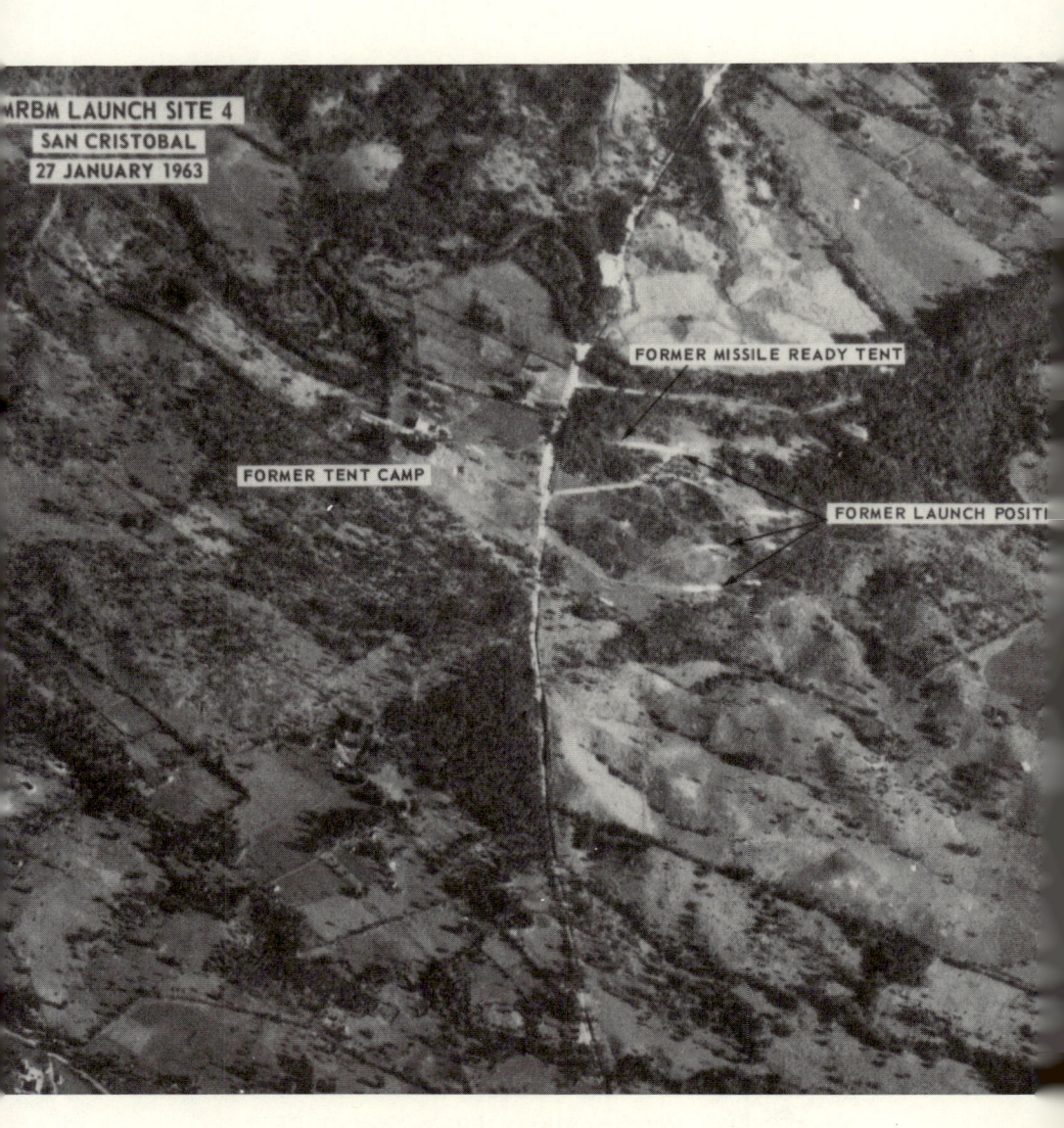

An aerial view of what had been a bustling military base at San Cristóbal, Cuba, three months after the Soviet Union agreed to remove its missiles.

buildup on the island. Then, on October 16, 1962, President Kennedy received photographs showing that bases were being constructed for missiles with a range capable of reaching many American cities.

President Kennedy reacted boldly. He said, "Those weapons constitute an explicit threat to the peace and security of all the Americas." He also pointed out that the presence of the missiles upset the nuclear balance between the East and West.

Then, with the approval of the Organization of American States (OAS), Kennedy ordered a blockade of all Cuba to prevent the landing of additional missiles that were now en route by sea from the Soviet Union. (The OAS, which was formed in 1948, is made up of twenty-eight Western Hemisphere countries. Its aims are to settle hemispheric disputes peacefully, provide protection for the member nations, and promote cooperation among them. Both Cuba and the United States are member nations.)

As the missile-carrying Soviet freighters were making their way across the Atlantic, the Kennedy order turned the Caribbean area into an armed and waiting camp. U.S. warships surrounded Cuba and dispatched aircraft to patrol its coasts. Florida and the Gulf ports were alerted and mobilized for any trouble that might come. Nuclear B-52 bombers took flight. Polaris submarines spread themselves out over the ocean. Intercontinental missiles stood in readiness.

Throughout the United States, the people held their collective breath. The world's two superpowers were about to confront each other openly. Would the Soviet supply ships turn back when ordered to do so by the blockading forces? Or would they press on? Would the confrontation be the spark that would detonate an American-Russian nuclear war?

For several days, the air was tense with the horrible possibility of war. The two nations, so long antagonistic because of their conflicting ideologies, seemed to be staring at each other, with each waiting for the other to give in. Then, when the supply ships were close to the Caribbean, Soviet Premier Khrushchev capitulated. He called for the ships to return home. He agreed to pull all the Russian missiles out of Cuba. In turn, Mr. Kennedy pledged not to invade Cuba if the missiles were removed.

A TRIUMPH, A SLAP IN THE FACE

The successful blockade was a triumph for President Kennedy—and a slap in the face for Castro. The news came out that Khrushchev had agreed to withdraw his ships and missiles after a series of negotiations with Washington. He had carried out the negotiations and reached his decision on his own. Not once had he consulted with Castro.

Humiliated at being ignored in a situation that had Cuba at its core, Castro tried to salvage some of his dignity and pride. The Kennedy-Khrushchev agreement called for United Nations inspectors to visit the missile bases to make certain that the weapons had been removed. Castro refused to allow the inspectors to enter the island. Through the use of air reconnaissance and aerial photography, however, the U.S. government satisfied itself that Khrushchev was living up to his agreement. Peace slowly returned to the Caribbean.

But the peace was on the surface only. Underneath, there was still trouble between Cuba and the United States. It was trouble that would continue through the 1960s and into the 1970s as Castro launched a campaign to make himself something more than his nation's leader. He set out to become a leader for the surrounding Latin American countries. These were countries that, because they were not yet as developed as the world's wealthiest and most influential nations, were said to be part of what was called the Third World.

TROUBLED NEIGHBORS

8

CASTRO'S FAILED DREAM

Castro launched his bid early to become the Western Hemisphere's Third World leader. Soon after overthrowing Batista—and well before the Bay of Pigs attack and the October missile crisis were ever dreamed of—Castro said that he wanted the Andes mountains of South America to be the Sierra Maestra of the future. It was his way of calling for an armed revolutionary movement that would engulf both South and Central America. He urged all Latin Americans to rise against their governments.

The Cuban leader accused those governments of oppressing the common people. Further, he charged that they were under the economic thumbs of the giant United States and other foreign powers. Then, in a speech given at Havana on July 26, 1960, the eighth anniversary of his attack on the Moncada Barracks, Castro pledged Cuba to the task of liberating Latin America.

By the time of that speech, the United States government was convinced that Castro was a Communist. Washington said that he had introduced communism into Latin

America by bringing it to Cuba and now intended to "export" it to his many neighbors. Committed to opposing communism wherever it appeared in the world, Washington set about trying to frustrate Castro's hopes of spreading it through the Western Hemisphere. The work in this direction saw the United States provide various Latin countries with millions of dollars in military and economic aid so that they were not only well prepared to meet the threat of revolution but also sympathetic to the American cause. And it saw the CIA develop the plan for the Bay of Pigs attack.

In other actions, the United States accused Castro of launching three revolutions from Cuban soil during 1959 and 1960. These were uprisings in the Dominican Republic, Panama, and Haiti. Hastily and poorly planned, all three uprisings were quickly put down. Specifically, Castro was charged with training the rebels, providing them with a few arms, and then granting them asylum in Cuba when the uprisings fell apart. Castro denied having anything to do with the Panamanian and Haitian revolts, but admitted to being involved in the Dominican Republic upheaval.

HIDDEN REASONS

Castro may have been seeking power and the spread of communism when he first called for armed revolutions throughout Latin America. But many historians say that there were also other, hidden reasons for the call.

To begin, as a Communist nation, Cuba was alone in the Western Hemisphere, located far away not only from the Soviet Union and its European satellites but also the Communist states in Asia. Castro needed—and was seeking to develop—neighbors of his political persuasion so that Cuba would have additional strength when dealing with the United States and other non-Communist countries.

The next reasons came in the months following his initial call and had to do with the Soviet Union. Ever since he had agreed to trade Cuban sugar for Soviet oil, Castro had received increasing help from the Russians. Lending him money and providing him with military equipment and specialists, the Soviet Union soon became as influential in Cuba's political and economic life as the United States had once been. The belief is that Castro felt that the Soviet Union might continue extending its influence to the point of taking direct control of the island. Castro wanted to be surrounded by Latin American Communist states that would oppose any takeover of a Latin friend by an outsider—even if that outsider was communism's founding nation.

Then, in the wake of the 1962 missile crisis, Castro had an additional worry. Soviet Premier Nikita Khrushchev, without even bothering to consult him, had backed down in the face of the Kennedy blockade. Castro wondered if he could count on the Soviet Union's help were Cuba ever invaded by some other outsider. Again, he had the need to be surrounded by Communist states loyal to him as the hemisphere's ranking Third World leader.

THE CALL FAILS

Castro's call, however, went ignored in most of Latin America. Some countries were content with their present governments. Many were receiving military and economic aid from the United States; this aid would have been lost had they installed Communist governments; they would have been forced to depend on help from the Soviet Union, a country they saw as far less able to provide all the funds they needed. Further, a number of the Latin nations had no love for Castro. This fact was pointed up when military groups overthrew four governments in the 1960s—Argentina and Peru in 1962, and Brazil and Bolivia in 1964.

On all occasions, the toppled regimes were replaced with governments hostile to the Cuban leader.

Even many Communist officials in the Soviet Union and Latin America did not like Castro's idea. They feared that it could lead to a bloodbath throughout the hemisphere. And they feared that armed revolts might well fail because they would have to be fought with guerrilla forces. Castro had successfully used guerrilla tactics, but he had been fighting a small army. They might well not work against governments boasting much larger armies.

All such concerns went for nothing because Castro's bid to become a Third World leader was suddenly and effectively thwarted in 1964. This happened when the members of the Organization of American States met in Washington, D.C., at the request of Venezuela. There, they heard the Venezuelan representative angrily say that fellow member Cuba had been detected shipping arms to revolutionary groups in his country.

The member nations, the United States among them, reacted to the charge with several actions. Although allowing Cuba to remain in the OAS, the members condemned the country, severed diplomatic relations, suspended all trade (except for foodstuffs and medical supplies), and cut off commercial air and sea transportation to and from the island. As a result, Cuba was isolated from all its neighbors except Mexico.

These actions were nothing new to the United States. Washington had broken off diplomatic relations with Cuba in 1961. A partial embargo had been placed on Cuban sugar in 1960, when Castro took over the American-owned refineries that refused to process his imports of Russian crude oil. That embargo had been extended to all Cuban trade in 1961—in the wake of the Bay of Pigs invasion. Then the missile crisis of 1962 had seen Washington outlaw commercial air and sea traffic to Cuba. To one degree or another, the U.S. embargoes and the travel ban are still in effect today.

Although thwarted by the OAS actions, Castro persisted in his call for armed revolutions. And, rather than behaving as if he were defeated, he expanded his aims. Within two years, Castro was working to become not only a Third World leader in Latin America but in Africa and Asia as well. In the meantime, Cuban-American relations continued to be as troubled as ever.

STRAINS OF THE 1960s

The troubles of the 1960s were several. Following the assassination of President John F. Kennedy in 1963, Americans everywhere were enraged on learning that his killer, Lee Harvey Oswald, had Communist ties and had once tried to go to Cuba for military training. (It was later learned that he had failed to gain entry because the Cuban authorities looked on him as dangerous.) A widespread rumor, never substantiated, held that Castro had been behind the assassination plot. Then came the following problems:

The Move Against Guantánamo Bay

In 1964, Castro's long-standing anger with the United States drove him to take an action against the naval base at Guantánamo Bay. Despite the animosity between the two governments, Castro had always said that he would honor Cuba's part of the 1934 treaty that, in dropping the hated Platt Amendment, leased the base indefinitely to the U.S. government. He had never demanded that the Americans leave, but now he seemed intent on driving them out. He closed off the fresh water supply to the base.

The base met the problem by first bringing in water by ship from the United States. Then it imported and installed equipment for transforming the Bay's salt water to fresh water. The base has manufactured its own fresh water ever since.

To this day, Castro has continued to honor the terms of the 1934 treaty. At present, as it has done through the years, the United States annually sends a check to Cuba in payment for the lease of the base. Cuba never cashes the checks.

The Vietnam Conflict

Cuba and the United States stood on opposite sides throughout the Vietnam conflict. Castro lashed out at Washington for intruding in an Asian problem and sending more than a million men to fight for the South Vietnamese. Cuba itself committed some twenty thousand troops to the North Vietnamese cause.

The Dominican Republic

In April 1965, President Lyndon B. Johnson ordered five hundred Marines to the Dominican Republic, where an uprising was trying to return a deposed left-wing president—Juan Bosch—to power. Johnson, who eventually sent thirty thousand U.S. soldiers to the little country, claimed that the outbreak was being staged by local Communists under Castro's direction. There were even rumors that Castro's trusted lieutenant, Che Guevara, was running the operation in the Republic.

The president's action marked the first time in forty years that the United States had militarily intervened in a Latin American uprising. Supposedly, the action was meant to protect the Americans trapped in the midst of the fighting. But Johnson's true intent—the protection of the dictatorial regime in power at the time against what he saw as something worse—became clear a few days later in a television address when he said:

"The American nations cannot, must not, and will not permit the establishment of another Communist government in the western hemisphere. . . . This is what our beloved President John F. Kennedy meant when, less than a week before his death, he told us, 'We in this hemisphere must also use every resource at our command to prevent the establishment of another Cuba in this hemisphere.' "

Although there were many rumors and charges of Communist participation in the failed Dominican uprising, they were in time either proved false or greatly exaggerated. No conclusive evidence was ever furnished by the CIA or the Federal Bureau of Investigation that Cuba and other Communist nations had supplied arms to the Dominican rebels, that the uprising had been directed from Cuba, and that Ché Guevara had directed the operation from inside the Dominican Republic.

ON THE AFRICAN AND ASIAN SCENE

In 1966, Castro took his first step toward becoming more than a Third World leader in the Western Hemisphere. He helped to form and then arranged to be given the leadership of the Solidarity Conference. This was an organization that was made up of Communist and socialist delegates from some eighty Asian, African, and Latin American nations, which met regularly to consider methods for advancing their cause and coordinating what the group called "wars of national liberation." Havana became the permanent site of the conference meetings, and Castro became a major figure in the international Communist movement. As such, he began to involve Cuba in Asian and African conflicts. Cuban troops were sent to Vietnam and then, in the early 1970s, to Angola in Africa.

Angola

In Angola, the Cuban troops assisted in a civil war that ended decades of Portuguese colonial rule in 1975 and brought a Marxist regime to power. That Communist government remains in power today, assisted by some thirty thousand Cuban troops and fifteen hundred Soviet military advisers as it fights a revolution led by Jonas Savimbi. In early 1986, Savimbi visited Washington, D.C., in search of American aid for his cause.

The Cuban participation in the Angolan revolt brought a new moment of stress between the United States and Cuba. At the time, the tensions between Washington and Havana had eased somewhat and talks were underway to reopen the diplomatic relations that had been severed by President Eisenhower. The United States, however, supported the Angolan government that was being overthrown, causing President Gerald Ford to tell Castro: withdraw your forces or forget about normalizing relations with the United States. Castro rejected the demand. The talks were broken off, with the result that U.S.-Cuban diplomatic relations have remained broken to this day.

Ethiopia

Next, in 1977, Castro assigned military and technical advisers to help train the army of Ethiopia's socialist, one-party government in the use of arms provided by the Soviet Union. When neighboring Somalia invaded Ethiopia in a dispute over a stretch of territory that both claimed to own, Castro ordered seventeen thousand Cuban troops to help repulse the attack. The order earned him the anger of many of his people. They felt he was doing nothing but endangering Cuban lives in a minor and far distant war. Castro committed no further men to the fighting, but did not remove the seventeen thousand already there. The Somalis were driven back into their own land and the Cuban forces stationed themselves on the border. For a number of years, the watchful Cuban presence there freed the Ethiopian army to continue battling a revolutionary movement in Eritrea, a region that has long sought to secede from Ethiopia.

An African Rebuff

His involvement in African affairs did not win Castro the wholehearted gratitude of the Third World. In fact, it earned him a quiet rebuff at a meeting of Third World nations held in the summer of 1978. There, Nigeria's President Olusegun Obasanjo gave a speech in which he spent a moment thanking the "Russians and their friends" for their support in Africa. But then he warned the Cubans and the Soviets not to remain too long and overstay their welcome, for then they would risk being seen as imperialist powers in Africa—powers that want to run the affairs of weaker nations and exploit the people. He made it clear that many Africans yearned as much to be independent of Cuba and the Soviet Union as Cuba had once yearned to be independent of Spain and then the United States.

POLICY CHANGES

By the early 1970s, Castro had stopped what the United States had now long called his "export of communism" through revolution, meaning that he had abandoned his attempts to inspire and trigger armed uprisings. Realizing that the "export" tactic was meeting with failure in Latin America, he replaced it with a policy of supporting existing revolutions. It was under this new policy that Castro sent his troops into Angola. It was under this policy that Castro advised and provided arms for the [Sandinista] rebels who in 1979 overthrew the long-standing regime of Anastasio Somoza in Nicaragua and replaced it with a socialist government. And it was under this policy that Castro has provided advice and arms for guerrillas who have long sought to overthrow the government in yet another Central American state—El Salvador.

The late 1970s were witness to yet another development in Castro's policies. He began to seek the friendship of his surrounding neighbors through what were described as humanitarian projects. Cuban workers built a needed fishing port for the little country of Guyana, which is located on South America's northeast coast. On the island of Jamaica, Cuban advisers helped to build schools, dams, and a water plant. Cuba gave a commercial fishing trawler to tiny Grenada—the Caribbean island's first—in

1979. Then some three hundred Cubans helped the Grenadians build an airport. According to the island's government, the airport was meant to encourage the tourist trade. At the time, Grenada was in the hands of a Marxist regime that had controlled it since 1979.

Washington viewed all the Cuban work as a Castro plot to win his various neighbors over to communism. Washington further charged that the construction workers at Grenada were actually Cuban soldiers and that the new airport there was really meant to serve as a Soviet air base in the Caribbean. If there was truth to all these accusations, then the Castro plot was one that failed. Guyana remains an independent republic within the free world. Jamaica is still a member of the British Commonwealth.

As for Grenada, the 1980s saw an uprising against its Marxist regime. In October, 1983, the Organization of Eastern Caribbean States (OECS) asked President Ronald Reagan to intervene militarily to quell the fighting and protect the lives of the American citizens trapped on the island. Late in the month, U.S. Marines and Rangers—assisted by a small force from six OECS countries—landed at Grenada, defeated government troops and Cuba's "construction workers" in sharp fighting, evacuated the American citizens, and helped to end the Marxist government.

TROUBLED NEIGHBORS

9

CUBA AND THE UNITED STATES TODAY

Our story of two troubled neighbors has at last brought us to the present. How do Cuba and the United States now feel toward each other? What is happening between them today? What does the future hold for their long-troubled relationship?

We close by answering these questions and by looking at the two countries individually and then together.

THE UNITED STATES

America's official attitude toward Cuba remains almost totally unchanged since the suspicion that Castro was a Communist became a certainty during President Dwight D. Eisenhower's administration. The six presidents who followed Eisenhower—John F. Kennedy, Lyndon B. Johnson, Richard M. Nixon, Gerald R. Ford, Jimmy Carter, and now Ronald Reagan—all continued the hard-line policy that Eisenhower established toward this Communist state.

For example, as you will recall from chapter seven, Mr. Eisenhower first broke off diplomatic relations with the Castro government on January 3, 1961. The relations remained severed until an attempt was made to repair them during a period of reduced Cuban-American tensions in the mid-1970s. But President Gerald Ford called the attempt off when Cuba dispatched some thirty thousand soldiers to assist in the revolution that brought a communist government to power in Angola.

Later, in 1977, during the Carter administration, Cuba and the United States signed an agreement to exchange some representatives, but without restoring full diplomatic relations. Then, in 1982, Castro asked for a further improvement in diplomatic relations, but was refused by President Ronald Reagan. Consequently, the Carter agreement is still in effect today, but full diplomatic ties between the two neighbors today remain a thing of the future.

On the commercial scene, the United States reduced its import of Cuban sugar as a retaliatory action when Castro and the Soviet Union entered their 1960 agreement to exchange oil and sugar. Then, when the missile crisis occurred in October 1962, the United States stopped completely its import of Cuban sugar. These actions severely damaged the Cuban economy.

Adding to the damage was the 1964 decision by the member nations of the Organization of American States (including the United States) to cut off all trade with Cuba, except for foodstuffs and medical supplies. The action was taken, as was explained in chapter eight, when Castro was accused of supplying arms for the overthrow of the Venezuelan government. Some of these embargoes remain in effect today and continue to do him damage. In recent years, however, Castro has managed to repair some of the harm. He has been able to reestablish diplomatic relations and resume trade with six of the OAS states.

Still another example: The U.S. suspended commercial air and sea travel to and from Cuba during the 1962 missile crisis, with the Organization of American States taking the same step as part of its 1964 action against the Castro government. The travel restrictions were eased somewhat in the next few years, but then were tightened again in the late 1970s when Castro became involved in revolutionary movements in Africa. In general, the United States today grants permission for Cuban travel only to news reporters, academic researchers, and people needing to visit the island for personal or family reasons. Washington cannot stop Americans from traveling to Cuba as tourists, but can put them on trial for violating a U.S. law forbidding any trade with or money spent in an "enemy" nation.

Today, as has been the case since he took office, President Ronald Reagan believes that Cuba continues to pose the threat of extending communism throughout the Western Hemisphere. He strongly supports the rebel forces seeking to overthrow the present Sandinista government of Nicaragua, charging that it took power with the help of Cuban troops and arms (with the arms coming to Castro from the Soviet Union). Conversely, Mr. Reagan supports just as strongly the present government of El Salvador in the war it has long waged with guerrillas. The president believes that the rebels do not represent an uprising by the Salvadoran people themselves but are Communist forces supplied with Cuban arms.

CASTRO AND CUBA

Anyone who looks at Castro and his Cuba today will be presented with a picture of sharp contrasts.

One side of the picture shows, for instance, that his promised land reforms, Social Security measures, and educational efforts have greatly benefited the Cubans. The educational efforts are especially noteworthy. Over the years, they have almost completely erased Cuba's illiteracy rate (formerly one of the highest in the world) after beginning with an energetic campaign that saw one hundred thousand young people spread themselves throughout the countryside and, on a one-to-one basis, begin teaching the peasant population to read.

On another successful economic front, Castro has built a thriving tourist trade for the island despite the U.S. and OAS restrictions on commercial travel there. Most tourists come from Canada and western Europe and are met with fine accommodations and colorful entertainments. There is the possibility that, in a few years' time, the Cuban tourist trade will equal or surpass the nation's sugar trade (which presently accounts for more than 83 percent of Cuba's exports) as a moneymaker.

The other side of the picture, however, reveals that Cuba has suffered continuing economic problems during Castro's quarter-century as its leader. Some of the problems have resulted from the embargoes levied against the nation by the United States and the Organization of American States. Others, especially those seen in the early days of his regime, can be traced to the business and governmental inexperience of Castro's ministers when they were first in office.

One especially troublesome economic problem has grown out of Cuba's association with the Soviet Union. Castro promised early that he would accelerate the growth of Cuba's industry. But, because of a 1965 agreement with Moscow, the acceleration has been slower than originally anticipated. In that year, the Soviets urged Castro to concentrate more on agriculture than on industry. Specifically, they asked him to concentrate on a new agricultural endeavor—the raising of cattle, a commodity sorely needed in the Soviet Union and its European satellites. Dependent as he was on Soviet financial support—and thinking that cattle ranching would be a new and profitable business for Cuba—Castro agreed to the plan. The decision not only damaged Cuba's industrial growth for years to come but also caused a split between Castro and his long-time friend, Ché Guevara. Guevara left Cuba and involved himself in revolutionary movements elsewhere, at last losing his life during a 1967 uprising in Bolivia.

Castro himself is sharply aware of Cuba's economic and industrial shortcomings. In a fiery three-hour speech delivered in early February 1986, he said that he was declaring war on the slowness with which some of the country's economic and social programs have been developing in recent times. He told his listeners that he would discharge government officials and workers found guilty of "laziness, incompetence, and irresponsibility." He said that Cuban leaders can no longer excuse their economic and social mistakes on inexperience—not after his government has been in power for twenty-seven years.

In another set of contrasts, Castro seems to be liked by many of his people and intensely disliked by others. His supporters look on him as a liberator, a champion of the common people, a father figure who scolds them on occasion for not working hard enough, and a fellow citizen who loves baseball, tours the countryside usually in a jeep rather than a limousine, and stops to listen to the problems of peasant farmers and villagers. An island that was continually torn by revolution from the Céspedes uprising in 1869 to Castro's victorious arrival in Havana in 1959 has been free of a major rebellion ever since. There have been reports of minor outbreaks, and reports of numerous attempts on Castro's life. The minor outbreaks have come to nothing. America's CIA, working in cooperation with anti-Castro exiles, has been charged with plotting some of the assassination attempts.

Conversely, the very number of Cubans who have fled to exile in the United States since Castro's victory leave no doubt that he is widely disliked in his homeland. The first exiles were, as was reported in chapter seven, supporters of the overthrown Batista regime. They were soon followed by thousands of people who accused the Castro government of being harsh and suppressive. Until commercial transportation to and from Cuba was suspended during the 1962 missile crisis, these people were allowed to leave the island legally. When the suspension took effect, the people then began smuggling themselves into the United States aboard anything from rafts to fishing boats, with Castro then infuriating Washington in 1980 by opening his jails and some mental institutions and urging their inmates to join the flow northward. In all, approximately 1 million Cubans (not including their children who were born here) have found refuge in the United States over the past quarter of a century.

There seems to be no doubt that the Castro government does repress its opponents. In 1984, the Reverend Jesse Jackson went to Cuba while campaigning for the U.S. presidency and arranged the release of both native-born and American prisoners—twenty-six in all. The Cubans were said to be political prisoners, whereas the Americans were serving sentences for such criminal offenses as drug trafficking. Various human-rights organizations in the United States have estimated that more than one thousand of Castro's opponents are presently held in prison.

A final set of contrasts shows Castro regarded as a Soviet pawn by the United States and other free-world countries because of his communism and his economic dependence on the Soviet Union. At the same time, many historians consider this outlook to be groundless. In their opinion, Castro is certainly a Communist but just as certainly not a Soviet pawn or "yes man." They substantiate their beliefs by pointing to his outspoken criticism of the Soviet invasion of Afghanistan in 1979. Castro also criticized the Communist suppression of the workers' unrest that swept Poland in the late 1970s and has continued into the 1980s.

CUBA AND
THE UNITED STATES

If Castro and Cuba present a picture of contrasts, then the very same thing can be said of his relations with the United States in the 1980s. Some relations between the countries are as strained as they have ever been. Some, however, hold a glimmer of promise for a better future for the two neighbors.

Cuban-American relations were especially strained by a speech that Castro gave while hosting a Havana meeting for some six hundred political figures, labor leaders, and visiting journalists. He infuriated the United States when he made a suggestion for all the South American nations that have borrowed money from U.S. and other foreign banks in recent years. His advice: repudiate these debts to nations that had long exploited Latin America and refuse to pay them.

(Note: Some of the Latin nations were already behind in their debt repayments, a situation that was causing severe problems for the U.S. banks holding the loans. Had Castro's advice been followed, it could have spelled disaster for the lending institutions.)

However, despite this speech and despite the fact that Cuba and the United States have long had such limited diplomatic relations, the two neighbors over the years have twice achieved a healthy cooperation. In the 1970s, after a number of U.S. commercial airliners had been hijacked and made to fly to Cuba, Castro and Washington reached an antihijacking agreement. In it, Castro agreed not to permit hijackers to land their captive aircraft in Cuba and find sanctuary there.

Then, in 1984, the two countries signed an immigration treaty. The treaty established an annual quota for Cubans wishing to enter the United States. The quota was set at three thousand immigrants per year. The treaty also called for Castro to take back the twenty-seven hundred mental

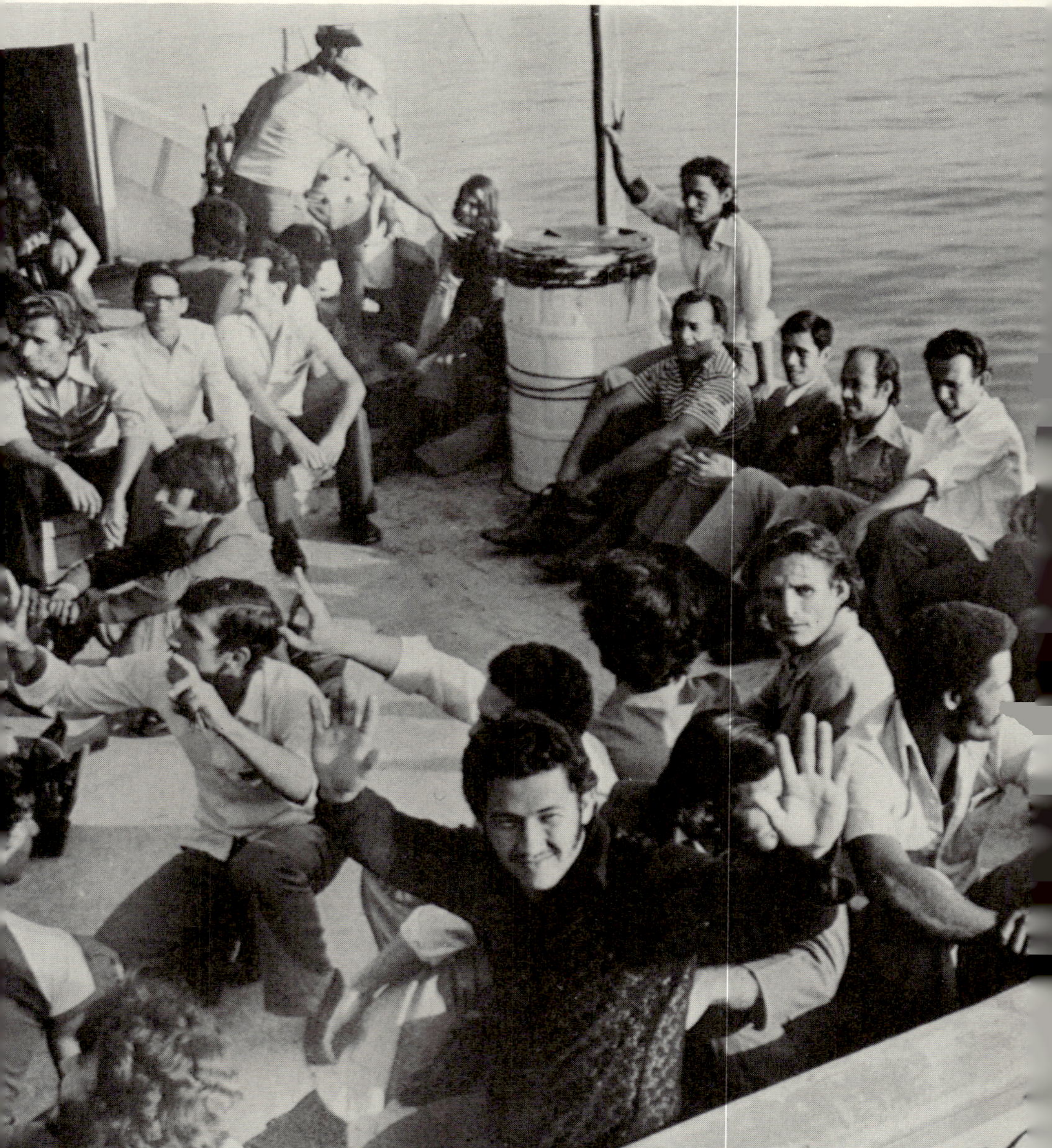

patients and criminals that he had deliberately released in 1980 so that they would come north to the United States as part of the Mariel boat lift.

But the contrasts that make up the picture of U.S.–Cuban relations are again to be seen. Castro allowed the antihijacking agreement to lapse after several years, and the immigration treaty was suspended in 1985 on Castro's orders, just a few months after being drafted. The reason for the suspension: Castro's anger over the U.S. sponsorship of an anti-Castro broadcasting station headquartered in the southern United States and called Radio Martí in honor of the great Cuban poet-revolutionary of the 1890s.

The United States and Cuba made an attempt to reinstate the suspended treaty late in 1985. The effort collapsed in July 1986 when the Cuban representatives demanded that the strength of certain U.S. radio channels be reduced so that broadcasts from Cuba could be more clearly heard on the North American continent. At the same time, the Cubans asked that Radio Martí limit the number of its broadcasts to their homeland.

Now, another contrast: Although these several efforts at cooperation ended in failure, Castro has shown an increasing willingness in recent years to coexist peacefully with the free world. This willingness was seen in 1977 when Cuban officials and the Carter administration reached their agreement for the limited exchange of diplomatic representatives. It was seen even more clearly in 1982 when Castro sought a further improvement in diplomatic relations but was refused by President Reagan. At that time, Castro offered to help end the Communist upris-

Cuban refugees wave and signal victory as they prepare to leave Mariel, Cuba, for the United States in April 1980.

ing in El Salvador, saying that he would withdraw his forces from the small country if the United States would end its support of the established government there. He admitted to having sent arms to the Salvadoran rebels, but said that the shipments had been stopped.

Further, the man who once called for armed revolutions throughout Latin America has of late offered a new kind of advice to the Communist government of Nicaragua. He suggests an economic and political cooperation with the free world. This is advice that runs exactly contrary to all his earlier calls for widespread uprisings. Why is it being offered? The belief is that Castro has realized there are dangers for any small country that becomes too dependent on a single large nation, as he did with the Soviet Union. The directions that the small country can then take are too few, whereas cooperation with the many nations of the free world offers a greater choice of direction and, thus, greater benefits for the small country.

A CHANGED MAN?

In all, in his dealings with the United States and the rest of the free world, Castro strikes many people as a man undergoing change—a change from an attitude of belligerency toward one's foes to one of peaceful coexistence with them. If he is actually undergoing such a change, it could be the result of any combination of factors.

It may have come about because his call for widespread armed revolution failed to set Latin America afire. It may have come about because, in his twenty-seven-year rule, Cuba managed to support only two successful Communist revolutions—the uprisings in Angola and Nicaragua. And it may have come about simply because Castro has grown older. There is now much gray in that famous beard and it may be that, with age, the angry revolutionary of old has slowly been transformed into the quiet, mature statesman who realizes that differences are best settled with talk and negotiations rather than with rifles and bloodshed.

But many people remain skeptical of Castro. They feel that, despite any outward appearance of quiet and cooperation, he continues to remain a man dedicated to the spread of communism throughout Latin America. At the time this book is being written, Washington continues to accuse him of aiding the Communist government in Nicaragua and supplying it with arms for its fight against the U.S.-supported Contra revolution. The tensions with which the two troubled neighbors have long lived remain.

On the other hand, the change that so many people see in Castro may actually be there. To them, it certainly seemed to be present in an interview of the mid-1980s with former U.S. diplomat Wayne S. Smith. Castro expressed the hope that Cuba and the United States would one day reach the point at which they can resolve their difficulties through talks and negotiated agreements. He then added:

"Someday our two countries will live in peace."

Did Castro mean what he said? Or was this an empty statement that he had no intention of remembering?

Time will tell.

RECOMMENDED READING LIST

If you would like to read more about Cuba, you will find the following materials to be of particular interest and help.

Books

Brennan, Ray. *Castro, Cuba, and Justice.* New York: Doubleday, 1959.

Carroll, Raymond. *The Caribbean: Issues in U.S. Relations.* New York: Franklin Watts, 1984.

Fagg, John E. *Cuba, Haiti, and the Dominican Republic.* Englewood Cliffs, N.J.: Prentice Hall, 1965.

Goldston, Robert. *The Cuban Revolution.* Indianapolis, Ind.: Bobbs-Merrill, 1970.

Halprin, Maurice. *The Rise and Decline of Fidel Castro.* Berkeley, Cal.: University of California Press, 1972.

Harman, Carter et al., eds. *The West Indies.* New York: Time-Life, 1972.

Hinckle, Warren and Turner, William R. *The Fish Is Red: The Story of the Secret War Against Castro.* New York: Harper & Row, 1981.

Johnson, Haynes with Artime, Manuel et al. *The Bay of*

Pigs: The Leader's Story of Brigade 2506. New York: Norton, 1964.

Kennedy, Robert F. *Thirteen Days: A Memoir of the Cuban Missile Crisis.* New York: Norton, 1969.

Langley, Lester D., ed. *United States, Cuba, and The Cold War.* Lexington, Mass.: D.C. Heath, 1970.

Lindop, Edmund. *Cuba.* New York: Franklin Watts, 1980.

Macauley, Neill. *A Rebel in Cuba: An American's Memoir.* Chicago: Quadrangle Books, 1970.

Matthews, Herbert L. *Revolution in Cuba.* New York: Scribner's, 1975.

Phillips, R. Hart. *Cuba: Island of Paradox.* New York: McDowell, Obolensky, 1959.

Plank, John, ed. *Cuba and the United States: Long Range Perspectives.* Washington, D.C.: Brookings Institution, 1967.

Robbins, Carla Anne. *The Cuban Threat.* New York: McGraw-Hill, 1983.

Tetlow, Edwin. *Eye on Cuba.* New York: Harcourt, Brace & World, 1966.

Thomas, Hugh. *Cuba: The Pursuit of Freedom.* New York: Harper & Row, 1971.

_____. *A History of the World.* New York: Harper & Row, 1979.

Williams, Byron. *The Continuing Revolution.* New York: Parents' Magazine Press, 1969.

Newspapers and Magazines

"Castro Calls for War on Incompetence." *San Francisco Chronicle,* February 5, 1986.

"Outcasts and Immigrants." *Time,* December 24, 1984.

Scobie, William. "Foreign Debt at Issue: Castro Asks Nations to Stiff U.S. for Billions." *San Francisco Examiner*, reprinted from *London Observer*, August 4, 1985.

Smith, Wayne S. "Cuba: Time for a Thaw?" *New York Times Magazine*, July 29, 1984.

INDEX

Italicized page numbers refer to illustrations.

Aguero, Andrés Riva, 81–82
Angola, 107–108, 109, 112
Arawak Indians, 12, 22

Batista, Fulgencio, 50, 55–56, *57*, 59–62, 63, 64, 66, 67, 70–72, 76–77, 79, 81–83
Bay of Pigs (1961), 91–93, *94*, 95–96
Bolivia, 115
Bosch, Juan, 106
Brú, Federico Laredo, 59
Buchanan, James, 29

Caffrey, Jefferson, 58

Campos, Arsenio Martínez, 31
Cardona, José Miro, 84, 85
Castro, Fidel
  Cuban invasion (1956), 68–69
  guerrilla leader, 69–70, *71*, 72–81, *82*, 83
  imprisonment and exile, 65–67
  and Latin America, 90, 101–105, 106–107, 109–110, 112–113, 119–121
  premier, 84–91, 113–116
  rebel leader, 64–65
  and Third World, 106, 107–109

Castro, Fidel *(cont.)*
See also Soviet/Cuban relations; U.S./Cuban relations
Castro, Raúl, 65, 69, 80, 85
Central Intelligence Agency (CIA), 93, 115
Céspedes, Carlos Manuel de, 30
Céspedes, Dr. Carlos Manuel de, 54
Columbus, Christopher, 11–13
Communism, threat to U.S., 73, 85–86, 87–91, 92–93, 96, 101–105, 106–110, 113
Cornwallis, Charles, 25
Coronado, Francisco Vásquez de, 16–17
Crowder, Enoch, 50
Cuba, history of
 Batista dictatorship, 55–63
 Castro dictatorship, 84–121
 Castro revolution, 63–70, *71*, 72–83
 European exploitation, 11–23
 independence, 47–50
 Machado dictatorship, 51–54
 Spanish-American War, 35–38, *39*, 40–41
 Spanish domination, 13, 18–20, 26–28, 30–32, 33
 U.S. domination, 41–47
Cuban constitution, 44–47, 51–52, 54, 61

De Grasse, François, 25
De Heredia, José María, 26
De León, Ponce, 15, 16–17
De Soto, Fernando, 16–17
Dominican Republic, 65, 83, 102, 106–107
Dorticós, Osvaldo, 88

Eisenhower, Dwight D., 78, 80–81, 87, 91, 108, 111–112
El Salvador, 109, 113, 120
Ethiopia, 108
European discovery of the New World, 11–17
Exiles, Cuban, 27, 53, 88, 89–90, 91–92, 93, 96, 115–116, 117, *118*, 119

Financial interests, U.S., 32–33, 41–43, 49–50, 52, 56–58, 73, 77–78, 80, 86–90, 104
Finlay, Carlos, 44
Ford, Gerald, 108, 112

Gómez, José Miguel, 47, 48–49, 59
Gómez, Miguel Mariano, 59
Gorgas, William G., 44
Grau San Martín, Ramón, 56–58, 61
Grenada, U.S. invasion (1983), 109–110

Guam, 40
Guantánamo Naval Base, 44–47, 48, 58–59, 80–81, 94–95, 105–106
Guevara, Ernesto "Ché," 67, 69, 70, 106, 115

Hawley-Smoot Act, 52, 58
Hearst, William Randolph, 37
Historia Me Absolvera, 66

Jackson, Jesse, 116
Jefferson, Thomas, 29
Johnson, Lyndon B., 106

Kennedy, John F., 95, 96–100, 105
Khrushchev, Nikita, 90, 100, 103

Lafayette, Marquis de, 25
Latin American/Cuban relations, 90, 101–105, 106–107, 109–110, 112–113, 119–121

Machado, Gerardo, 50–54
McKinley, William, 32, 33, 37, 38, 40
Mariel boat lift, 92, 116, 117, *118*, 119
Martí, José, 41, *42*
Mason, John Young, 29
Matthews, Herbert, 72–73
Mendieta, Carlos, 58–59
Menocal, Mario García, 47, 49,

Mexico, 13, 16, 66–67
Missile crisis (1962), 96, *97, 98*, 99–100

Nicaragua, 93, 109, 113, 120, 121

Obasanjo, Olusegun, 109
Organization of American States (OAS), 99, 104–105
Organization of Eastern Caribbean States (OECS), 110, 112, 113
Ostend Manifesto, 29
Oswald, Lee Harvey, 105

Palma, Tomás Estráda, 47
Panama, 44, 102
Philippine Islands, 38, 40
Pierce, Franklin, 29
Platt, Orville, 45
Platt Amendment, 45–47, 53, 58–59, 77
Prío, Carlos, 62, 67–68
Puerto Rico, 13, 15, 38, 40
Pulitzer, Joseph, 37

Radio Martí, 119
Reagan, Ronald, 110, 112, 113
Reed, Walter, 43–44
Roosevelt, Franklin, 53
Root, Elihu, 45

Savimbi, Jonas, 107
Slavery, *12*, 20–22, 28–30, 31

Smith, Earl T., 88
Smith, Wayne S., 121
Solidarity Conference (1966), 107
Somalia, 108
Somoza, Anastasio, 109
Soulé, Pierre, 29
Soviet/Cuban relations, 89, 90, 103, 114–115, 116
Spanish-American War, 35–38, *39*, 40–41

Ten Years' War, 30–32
Treaty of Paris, 40–44
Trujillo, Rafael, 65, 83

United Nations, 90
U.S./Cuban relations
   annexation proposal, 28–30
   Bay of Pigs, 91–93, *94*, 95–96
   during American Revolution, 24–25
   Grenada invasion, 109–110
   Guantánamo Naval Base, 44–47, 48, 58–59, 80–81, 94–95, 105–106
   Mariel boat lift, 92, 116, 117, *118*, 119
   missile crisis, 96, *97*, *98*, 99–100
   present day, 111–121
   Spanish-American War, 35–38, *39*, 40–41
   U.S. intervention, 32–34
   U.S. protectorate, 41–44
USS *Maine*, 33–35, *36*, 37–38
U.S./Soviet relations, 96–100
Urrutia, Manuel, 84, 86, 88

Washington, George, 25
Welles, Sumner, 53, 59
Weyler, Valeriano, 32
Wilson, Woodrow, 49
Wolham, Park, 80–81
Wood, Leonard, 41–43

Zayas, Alfredo, 47, 49–50